DIY PR

The Small Business Guide to 'FREE' Publicity

Penny Haywood

B. T. BATSFORD LIMITED · LONDON

Batsford Business Online: www.batsford.com

Published by B T Batsford Ltd,

583 Fulham Road,

London SW6 5BY

Batsford Business Online: www.batsford.com

Printed by

Redwood Books

Trowbridge

Wiltshire

ISBN 0 7134 8369 5

A CIP catalogue record for this book
is available from The British Library

INTRODUCTION

Publicity is the oxygen of business. If people don't know about your business, it will not survive. Yet small companies consistently neglect a free way of promoting themselves: using Public Relations (PR) to get free editorial coverage in newspapers and on radio and TV. It's a method used by all successful companies and once you know how, it's relatively easy to get effective free publicity.

Business journalists agree that small businesses often generate more interesting stories than corporations with professional PR representation. They can grow more dramatically, and invent interesting new products and solutions. But journalists rarely hear from small businesses or, if they do, the small businesses go about it in the wrong way.

Hiring a PR professional can be expensive but *DIY PR* will show you how to do it yourself. It will show you how to get your business in front of thousands of people without spending large sums on advertising. The Press Release Templates chapter includes ten common small business news scenarios plus notes, templates and examples of press releases. You don't need fancy equipment or big budgets, although access to word processing, photocopying and a fax will save a lot of time. Much PR practice is common sense, but it's amazing how common sense seems to be much easier with hindsight. If you follow the advice here, you will save a lot of effort.

The primary aim of DIY PR is to enable every reader to use PR techniques effectively to boost their business. We cover how to stir up media interest, and how to cope with it when you do, with tips on handling press interviews.

Reputation
However, press relations is just one PR technique. PR is much more. It's the art of managing your most precious business asset: reputation.

Without a reputation, you can't trade. Reputation, or to be more correct, *managed reputation,* is becoming so important that many US banks will not arrange loans without a PR plan in the business plan. That is why a chapter on PR Planning is included, along with a section on the more sales-related Marketing Plan.

Sometimes press relations is not the most effective PR technique. This is certainly true if you have very limited time, or a very limited range of potential customers. Nor would press relations be a wise move if you have a problem to sort out before you raise your public profile. The PR Plan chapter, plus the chapter on PR techniques (other than press relations) will help you decide whether, for example, sponsorship, awards or corporate hospitality would be a better way to boost your business.

Fundamentally, this book is about something far more important than short-term business boosting. It is to equip small business owners with the tools to manage their business reputation. For without reputation, no business can survive.

The author
Penny Haywood has over 25 years' PR experience, including 13 years' work with a bank. She has run her own small business for the past 11 years, and has managed successful DIYPR courses for small businesses since 1987. This book is based on these courses and she has received feedback from participants.

Feedback
Your experiences of using this book are important and feedback can be addressed to Penny Haywood at the address opposite. Or you can e-mail the author direct on penny_haywood_pr@compuserve.com.

DIYPR courses and press lists
Penny Haywood is available to run half-day DIYPR Press Relations or full day DIYPR Reputation and Press Relations courses for business groups. Penny Haywood PR can also provide starter press lists and specialised

trade press lists by e-mail or post. Contact Julia Deeprose for fees for courses and lists at:

Penny Haywood PR,
Communications House,
3 Lower Joppa,
Edinburgh,
EH15 2ER,
UK

http://ourworld.compuserve.com/homepages/Penny_Haywood_PR

Dedication

To Dougie, without whom my dishes would have turned green and furry during the writing of this book

Contents

Introduction

CHAPTER 1

WHAT IS PR?

PR stands for *Public Relations*. What does that mean?
Basically, it means what it says: PR is about managing your business'
Relations with its *Public*.

The PR Plus

PR – a *managed reputation* – brings you a number of positive benefits

- Customers will think more of you
- You will have more credibility with financial backers and the bank
- You will be in a better bargaining position with suppliers
- You will be able to attract better staff
- You will find it easier to keep existing customers
- A good reputation will encourage referrals and bring in new
  business

How do you achieve a good business reputation? Ultimately, reputation is
the sum total of what everyone connected to your business does or says
and what others say about your business.

Communicating consistent messages ('all singing from the same hymn
sheet') is the essence of all good communications practice. It helps to
develop memorable key messages about your products or services and

your business. Messages that everyone can be encouraged to use. These key messages can be repeated as 'tag lines' on your stationery, literature and will be used by you and your staff. They will also be repeated on all communications with the media. To work effectively, they have to be simple, easily memorable and easy to say.

How does PR manage reputation? It's a simple 3-step process: IPD

1. **Identify** which groups of people you need to reach to achieve your business objectives.
2. **Plan** how to get key positive messages to these groups as clearly and memorably as possible
3. **Deliver** key messages to their target audience or 'publics'.

At its best, PR gets your business messages across to thousands of people free of charge as editorial mentions and broadcast interviews. Used well, PR will raise your public profile and get you closer to the key people you want to influence.

Reputation

What exactly is this reputation PR techniques will manage?

All businesses have a reputation, whether they use PR to manage it or not. People do not want to deal with businesses that have lost credibility. This applies to any kind of business, from a consultancy or service provider, to a manufacturer, wholesaler or retailer.

Even a corner shop will suffer if word gets out that the change given is sometimes short, complaints about faulty goods are not being handled well, or that hygiene standards have slipped.

Of course, if there's something wrong with the product, no amount of promotion or PR will fix it. All things being equal, price, product/service quality plus customer care and delivery are essential. But reputation will be the decisive factor in a major sale.

Businesses cannot survive without reputation. If you do not believe me, just think what happened to Ratners, the UK high street jewellery chain. A few years ago the Ratners founder and chairman was widely reported in the media as having said their products were cheap because they were cr*p. Sales plummeted overnight and Ratners ceased to be a name in the High Street. All because the business had lost its reputation.

It's easy to see the effects of reputation on large businesses in the public eye, but small businesses that gain a reputation for cheating customers or failing to deliver will go bust just as fast. That is why banks often refuse to lend on the strength of a bulging order book. They know quality and customer service will suffer if a firm expands too fast and the resultant loss of reputation spells the end of their loan repayments.

Too few small businesses make a conscious effort to manage the very reputation that enables them to survive, which is a bit like driving down the freeway blindfold: highly dangerous and definitely not recommended.

The press greatly magnifies a business reputation – or its lack of one, as we saw in the Ratners case. That is why a planned approach to press relations is important and a chapter on making a PR plan for your business takes you through the process.

Having a good reputation will benefit every aspect of your business, from finding it easier to hire and retain staff, through to motivating employees, agents, retailers, license holders, or franchisees. With a good reputation, it's easier to find backers, borrow money and negotiate with suppliers. And you will find it easier to attract and retain customers.

The importance of PR and business reputation is being increasingly recognised. Many American banks now want to see a PR Plan in addition to a Marketing Plan as standard elements in the business plan before they will lend. Where America leads, Britain usually follows.

Clear messages

A lot of PR is about information-provision: sending out positive information that is clear, and not easily misunderstood. Obviously, press reports reach more people than individual word of mouth reports. It's worth remembering that, although powerful, there are limits to what PR can do with the press. Information provision must be based on communicating the truth.

In the case of the business founder calling the core products rude names in public, there is not an awful lot that PR can do beyond damage limitation and a swift name change. But a name change is no good unless the core problem is solved. Loss of reputation will follow a business around, no matter how many times it changes its name.

Repercussions of negative publicity can become surprisingly wide. I would not be surprised if people in the UK look more closely at the quality of high street jewellery since the Ratners debacle, even though it happened years ago. I know I do.

What 'publics'?

Looking at the 'public' in Public Relations, most people assume this means the general public. However, reaching the entire general public of an entire nation is hard work, and unnecessary effort. Most businesses can break down their potential audience into specific categories that directly impact on their business. Once you have identified these groups, it becomes easier to focus on ways to reach them. That is why identifying your 'publics' is one of the first steps towards developing your own PR Plan.

I like to think of a business as having several 'publics'. That is several groups of people whose good opinion is vital to the smooth operation of the business. Some 'publics' are obvious. Indeed, some are so obvious that they are typically neglected by small businesses – with adverse consequences as a result.

The first step in creating your own PR Plan is to select from the following list, the 'publics' that impact on your business. Typical 'publics' that are important to small businesses include:

(In a rough suggested order of importance, although this will vary according to your business)

- **Customers:** without their goodwill, there is no business future.
- **Potential customers:** without them, there will be no future business.
- **Staff:** without people, the business cannot function – even if it's only you at the moment (this could well come first on many PR lists).
- **Suppliers and contractors:** without their willingness to supply you, your business cannot make or do anything.
- **Advisers:** without them to keep you legal and tax efficient, you could go out of business.
- **Investors, bankers, backers or shareholders:** without them, many businesses would fail. Even if it's only the potential for a small overdraft facility at the bank, or a loan from friends or family to tide you over a rough patch.
- **Family or immediate circle:** without their support, business life could be very difficult.
- **Friends:** without their help, few business people could cope.
- **Neighbours:** without their co-operation, you could be forced out of business.
- **Authorities and regulatory bodies:** without their goodwill, they could spell the end of your business.
- **Local community:** without their goodwill, business is a struggle.
- **Competitors:** help to stimulate demand in your market sector. They

can be a surprisingly good source of business (see below).

- ■ **Opinion formers:** in all business and industrial sectors there are those whose expert opinion is sought, whether it's for resolving disputes or giving general comment in the media. Their support confers extra status on your business.
- ■ **Potential recruits:** without them you would be unable to cope with growth and staff replacement.
- ■ **The media:** can carry your messages to almost all the groups on this list.
- ■ **Trade unions:** if they are a traditional force in your line of business.
- ■ **Local and national government:** if they are intending to change the regulatory framework in a way that will impact on your business. Business rates and taxes, for example, or employment legislation, health and safety or environmental issues.

Most of the categories of these 'publics' are obvious, but some people question having 'friends', 'family', or 'competitors' identified on a formal PR plan as audiences they are trying to reach. In addition, small businesses often neglect to keep investors informed about the progress of their businesses.

Let us look at the thinking behind these particular categories in more depth.

Competitors

Take competitors, for instance. They are a mixed blessing. Obviously, they are a threat. But their sales activities stimulate the market and there is strength in numbers. If you are in the sort of business where a competitive pitch is normal before a supplier is appointed, a competitor's good idea may well benefit you. The buyer has to put it out to tender and you could get the chance to pitch for business that was inspired by a main competitor.

The most obvious example of competitive business stimulation is the clustering of competing retail outlets. London's Tottenham Court Road is the UK's hi-fi and computer shop Mecca, where scores of shops compete. Prices are the keenest you will find and it's the spot where clued-up customers go if they do not want to buy by mail order.

Everywhere you go, you will see this clustering phenomenon. Restaurants group together to create a dining-out magnet in an area. Banks and building societies cluster in High Streets. Clothes shops cluster in malls and main thoroughfares.

Designers, illustrators and artists congregate, attracting related art and graphic supply shops, advertising agencies and reproduction houses who turn artwork into the colour proofs and film which printers use. All backed-up by trendy bistros, wine bars and cafés.

The City of London is a square mile of financial clustering.

Clustering is recognition of the fact that few, if any, individual businesses can cater for all needs or tastes, all the time. There are horses for courses, different choice of products, services and range of expertise, different levels of back-up services, different guarantees and prices. Offer the customer a good selection of businesses in a particular area and customers will go to that area because they know they will get a far greater choice.

Clustering is generally good for business, provided you cluster with the best. Even if you are working from home, you could benefit from virtual clustering with competitors in certain areas of the Internet.

A trade directory is a kind of all-embracing trade or professional cluster.

The PR value in competitors is that they are the people closest to you in terms of understanding the business. If your industry is hit by a common threat, it makes sense to stand together and lobby against it. Whether lobbying is done through a relevant professional association or a local informal network will depend on the nature of the threat. The important thing is to make sure your voice is heard.

Your reputation amongst your peers is important. Professional respect may lead to a mutual referral system where you pass on to each other business you cannot cope with.

In time, forging business links with competitors may lead to very successful joint ventures which neither party could have handled individually; or you may take over someone else's business when they retire.

Friends and family

Friends and family are the people who should most want to support you. Big businesses recognise that the support of family and friends benefits their business. They spend a great deal of time and effort on family open days and special events. That way, children and partners can see where parents work; and hear what the company is doing, and why.

For small businesses, there is no need for vast expense, but you do need to secure the understanding of those around you. Yet I have met wives and husbands who, for want of proper information about their partner's business, hold the enterprise back, or miss golden opportunities to give the business a boost.

It's tempting to keep one area of your life apart from business, so that you can completely relax, but the penalty for doing so could be very high. The trouble is, you do not know what you could be missing until you start keeping friends and family informed.

Friends and family case study:
Unaware of wife's business potential

One wife I met had not got a clue about her husband's business, despite the fact that it was their only source of income. In fact, the business was doing reasonably well. It would do a lot better if the biggest corporation in the area could be persuaded to switch allegiance from a larger but more remote supplier. The business could match, but not beat, the bigger company's prices and quality; but by being on the spot, they were confident they would be able to give a much better service.

The husband had been trying for months to see the key corporate buyer, completely unaware that his wife was in the same tennis club as the buyer's wife. Actually, the two women got on really well and had teamed up as doubles partners. The husband had never bothered to mention at home that breaking into that corporation was his main sales target. The wife never thought to mention her new friend's husband, although she knew the company for which he worked.

It eventually came out at a business reception to which spouses were invited. Once the couples had met socially, it was easy to fix up an appointment. The business was won, but months of lost sales opportunities had been wasted.

Friends and family case study:
The caterer who could not cook the books

Another situation I encountered was the husband who advised his wife to keep her business within certain income brackets to avoid registering for VAT. He was completely unaware of the business potential she was sitting on. Other business advisers tell me this situation's not uncommon. I only found out because I was chatting to the wife, who ran an outside catering business, when someone offered her a lucrative contract. But she turned it down. I could not resist asking why, since she made delicious food and I had been on the point of asking for her business card myself.

I was told she was turning work down all the time because she must not exceed the VAT threshold. She was astonished to hear I had registered voluntarily for VAT from day 1 of starting my business so I could claim the VAT back on my set-up expenses.

The outside caterer had a niece with relevant qualifications who was already working part-time for her. The niece wanted to come into the business full-time. They even had the space to expand within their existing premises. The only thing stopping them from accepting enough work to create a proper job for the niece was the dread of handling all the VAT paperwork.

She was persuaded that a good book-keeper would keep her straight on VAT and relieve her of the paperwork she hated.

Fortunately, the person who offered her the work kept the offer open. The caterer decided to go for it, spreading the word through word of mouth, encouraging referrals, and getting a write-up in the local paper. Quoting the write-up in a subsequent mailshot, she sent it to local businesses. The quote was also used in a flyer distributed to local houses.

The caterer now employs her niece plus three friends and works with a freelance book-keeper. They adjust hours to suit themselves and everyone involved has benefited.

She is receiving more press coverage by launching all-in catering packages as niche products: the wedding lunch package, the business reception package, the business lunch pack. All launches are spearheaded by a press release and follow-up phone calls, along with letters and calls to customers and to people who recently made enquiries to the business.

With all that potential, why hadn't she grown her business sooner? The husband had given her the advice to steer clear of VAT in the early stages because he knew she wasn't good with figures and it was too early to employ a book-keeper. No-one had thought to update the decision.

The husband was very busy himself and genuinely had no idea of the amount of work she was turning down. His wife had not thought to mention it to him, probably through an exaggerated fear of the extra VAT burden she thought success would bring.

WHAT IS PR?

Many small business owners will have experienced the third-party phenomenon, where business comes to you in a roundabout way through a third-party recommendation. Some consultancy businesses rarely seem to get business any other way! Why?

People like making recommendations. They like to show they know people who can make things happen. And it works because people prefer to do business with personal connections. But you need to make sure you get clear messages across, to make it easy for them to recommend you.

Friends and family case study:
The tempting temp

I once won a plum job from a major competitor following a conversation with a temp in a client's office. The temp surfaced a couple of years later in a full-time job with a rapidly-expanding company. When her company were seeking to renew a contract to produce their customer magazine, she recommended adding me to the pitch list because she knew we had a publishing arm. How did she know? Quite simply, because I had told her.

When I asked her why she'd recommended me, she said I was the only one that had treated her like a human being and not 'just a temp' all that time ago.

When asked what I do, it's easy to say "I run a PR company" and leave it at that. No-one's quite sure what PR is, and the conversation takes another turn.

But I always say "I run a PR and publishing company for boosting business". It's only a few more words but there is no doubt about what I basically do and it gives people an opening to ask "What do you mean? Boosting business?" Or they may pick up on the publishing angle. In any case, I'm up and running, telling them more about my business and finding out about theirs.

Yes, I train small businesses in DIYPR, and yes I train people in publication management. But these are variations on the PR and publishing theme. Of course, if I know someone is interested in the training side, I would lead with that, but at least I know what rule I am breaking.

Even when you don't know people well, they are still likely to recommend you, provided they have a fair idea of what you do. You do not have to be false about it, but you do need to develop a well-chosen short sentence or two. It needs to contain specific memorable references to what your business does, so that can be easily passed on in the course of conversation.

Then, instead of answering "Fine" when someone asks "How's it going?", you will be able to say "Great, we've broken into the finance sector at last", (or whatever geographical or industrial sector you care to name). If the reply is "I didn't know you were into finance (or whatever)... " the chances are they will start making connections for you there and then.

Just remembering to drop a few short, easily memorable comments or updates on your business will make networking much more effective, and ensure you pick up the opportunities that are all around you. You may not even need to resort to press relations if you hone your networking skills. But networking will help refine your key messages, and that is important when you come to dealing with the press. Here is how it works:

WHAT IS PR?

We are trained every day to communicate clearly with the spoken word. People give definite face-to-face signals when they are bored. If you practise developing spoken communication messages, you will always end up with more focused and clearer messages than if you start with the written word. In fact, it's a good idea to imagine you are telling a friend about a product or service if you want to find clear simple ways of describing it. Develop the knack of listening to yourself putting the case in face-to-face meetings.

Developing the ability to boil down key activities into simple messages is vital when dealing with the press. A busy newsroom will give you about five seconds to make your point, whether it's on paper or on the telephone. So it's good to practise improving 'clear message' skills whenever you can.

Do not try and give a convoluted catch-all description of everything you do. One new business owner I saw being interviewed for a small business survey said he was into marketing one minute and hiring cars the next. He did not seem to know much about either and I concluded that if he did not know what he was doing, no-one else did. It's possible he was very good at something but I was not waiting to find out what.

Knowing what you want to say, then saying it clearly and concisely, builds inner confidence. Confidence about what you do inspires respect and, in turn, boosts that fragile flower called reputation. It's a positive spiral, so tap into it.

Don't worry if you don't get all your messages across. Prioritise and get one important message over. If people are interested, there will be time enough to tell them more about your activities. Start with your speciality, or your current projects. The important thing to realise is that you can only get across the flavour of what you do. But that may be enough.

Phrases like:

"I'm a management consultant for utility companies". It's easy for someone to pass this on with something like "He's Harry, he's a consultant to big utility companies. Hey, don't you work with an electricity company?"

"I'm a florist. We do business seminars as well as bouquets", might be passed on as "Jane's a florist. You know, she might be able to help you with that big seminar you're doing. She does business functions as well as weddings."

"We do designer hairdressing at down-to-earth prices", could be translated into "I know someone who might be able to help you with that fashion show you were talking about. She's a designer hairdresser but her prices are reasonable."

"We sell top designer labels for a fraction of their original price", could become "You can get designer clothes for pennies at her shop."

"We do guaranteed wood floors and fitting", could become "Hey, weren't you talking about getting a hard wood floor? I know an outfit that does guaranteed wooden flooring, and they'll fit it, too."

"We're accountants specialising in reducing tax bills for small businesses," might be passed on as "Why don't you speak to John – he'll tell you how to pay less tax."

Even if people you meet do not seem remotely connected to your business world, make sure they know what you do.

A remote aunt may play bridge with the mother of a potential customer and you have got no way of knowing there is a potential connection unless you prime her.

A partner may meet someone who makes just the thing you have been looking for – if you have mentioned it to her.

A child may be friends with someone whose parents are influential in the health department that is been causing you all sorts of problems through a simple misunderstanding. An informal chat could clear the air.

It is said that no-one in the world is more than six personal connections away from anyone else. Go on, try it and see how far you can get.

Investors

Another class of 'public' that gets strangely ignored by smaller business, is the investor or financial backer. Since these are the guys that can pull the plug on your business, you will not find many big businesses making this mistake. Indeed, whole investor relations departments and specialists are hired to look after this one type of person. But surely small businesses do not have to bother?

Well, try to increase your overdraft facilities or borrow money to replace a broken computer, or car, if you have not kept your bank manager in the picture. It does not take much. A note or 'phone call just to let him know when you have had a business success. A quick check to see he has all the information he needs, even if you do not need to borrow.

Similarly, if you know you are heading for a rough patch, let backers know you may need to borrow before you desperately need to be bailed out. That way, you will look as if you know what you are doing and you will have time to pull together any information they request without chewing the carpet over the delays.

Send your bank manager, and any backers, copies of your year-end figures, even if they are not great. At least you will be put in the category that is labelled "Keeps me in touch" instead of "Complete mystery. I wonder if our money's safe?"

Even if your backer is a friend or family member, put yourself in their shoes. Wouldn't you like to know whether the business you had helped is doing OK? It will not take long: a quick call or comment when you do well will keep them feeling comfortable. A timely warning if you are heading for a rough patch will give you a chance to negotiate a planned repayment holiday instead of leaving them short at the last minute. You are more likely to be able to borrow again if you take your backers along with you.

PR SUCCESS TASK No 1

Make a list of your 'publics', using the list on pages 5 and 6 as a prompt, and add other 'publics' whose support is relevant to the smooth running of your business.

Now list what you have done over the last 12 months to keep them informed of your activities.

Ask yourself: do all your key 'publics' know what your business does? What your most successful products or services are? Whether you are doing well? Who you would most like to have as new customers? What your targets are for next year?

The answers to these questions are a good start for your PR Plan.

PR SUCCESS TASK No 2

Write down the spoken phrase you use most often to answer the question "What do you do?" Could it be more informative or clearer? Refining messages about your business is something you will need to be able to do in more detail in the press relations section. Start honing these communication skills now.

CHAPTER 2:

THE PR PLAN

While good PR will help spread the word, there is no use stirring up demand you can't fulfil, or raising your profile when you are not in shape to cope with the consequences. More importantly, your PR objectives must match your overall business goals. Otherwise your PR activities will pull you seriously off course. That is why a planned approach is essential.

The PR plan comes with four tools:

1. **The PR questionnaire,** specially devised for small businesses
2. **The PR techniques symbols and checklist** with symbols devised specially for this book, allowing you to see at a glance what each technique will do, and the resources you will need to achieve results.
3. **The PR techniques by results chart** for use in choosing the techniques you need to achieve the results whether it is:
    - ✓ a sales boost
    - ✓ greater prestige so you can put up prices or be more selective over customers
    - ✓ a higher public profile, leading to easier sales, recruitment and dealings with the relevant authorities and other bodies.
4. **The restricted resources list** for use in honing your chosen PR techniques list to suit the resources at your disposal:

- time
- money
- contacts book or database
- IT skills and computer.

Use these four tools to focus on what you want to achieve with PR, and align PR to your main business goals.

The value of PR

If you have any doubts about the worth of PR to your business, recent research into business reputation valued it as being worth approximately a year's turnover.

(Source: What Price Reputation, Manchester Business School).

51% of those polled during the study agreed that "improving reputation improves profits".

Mirage or reality?

The same study divided company reputation into three elements:

- **Personality:** the characteristics that make a company what it is
- **Image:** the way the company packages itself
- **Identity:** the impression others have of the company

It's a useful distinction to think about if you are trying to nail a credibility problem. Try and find out as much as you can about your business personality, image and identity. Is your business hard/soft, lean or generous? Friendly and approachable? Cool and professional? Expert and remote? Vibrant and expansive? Detail orientated and perfectionist? Hi-tech or people-orientated? Youthful enthusiasm or elder statesman? Safe and reliable? Bold and daring? Leading edge or steady? Doggedly persistent or flashes of inspiration? Team-led or full of prima donnas? You will no doubt add your own traits to the list.

There are no rights and wrongs here. All are valid, positive qualities in certain business areas. Some businesses will have apparently conflicting traits embodied in different people. The important thing is to explore the overall perception.

Think hard about the personality, image and identity. If they don't match exactly, there is a credibility gap you need to address. For example, if the personality does not fit the perceived identity, you will be seen as peddling a mirage.

PR and Marketing

The marketing plan shows how you intend to sell a specific product or service: its price, position in the marketplace, how it will be distributed and how each individual product or service is to be promoted.

The PR plan covers general business reputation, its key messages (including sales messages), the audience you are targeting and the techniques you will use to deliver these messages.

THE PR PLAN

The PR plan crosses into marketing when PR techniques such as press relations are used in a sales support role to promote individual products and services. However, press relations also carries general PR messages about the business, which is why press relations remains primarily a PR rather than a marketing function.

PR techniques

To keep you focused on results you can expect from PR, and the resources you will need to practise various PR techniques, we have devised symbols to help you. You will find more information about PR techniques in Chapter 4.

You will see there is a provision for including costs in PR activity. In a book devoted to free publicity, the primary focus is on press relations which can be practised quite effectively for little more than basic telephone, stationery and postage costs. That press publicity should eventually generate enough business to enable you to branch out into other methods of promoting your business. If you are going to spend money on related communications materials and techniques, you will get better value for money if you focus the expenditure on your key business objectives as part of an overall plan.

Where the **£/$** symbol appears, this generally denotes relatively small amounts, delivering good value for money in comparison to the equivalent advertising spend.

££/$$ denotes a more serious sum. Only the individual business owner can weigh up whether their particular situation demands that expense.

Where **£/$ ££/$$** appears together, you should have a choice of finding a low cost option, or spending heavier amounts.

The other resource few small business owners have in abundance is time.

If a PR activity is low on cost, it's likely to be high on time. The ⏱ symbol means you have to invest time and effort to achieve results. Press relations is particularly time-intensive. However, it's also remarkably effective when you consider that every reporter can influence thousands of readers. How long would it take to get your message out to that size of audience by any other means?

Given the importance of your business reputation, you have to make the choice as to whether to devote time or money to ensuring your long term business survival.

The good news is that it *is* possible to gain powerful press publicity without vast cash outlays. There are few other cashless publicity options apart from word-of-mouth which, of course, does not have the mass reach of the press.

PR SUCCESS ACTION: The right choice of PR techniques will vary from business to business. What works for one will not necessarily work for another. It's worth trying the less expensive PR techniques over a longer period, as the effect is cumulative. You will need about six months to gauge how press relations will work for your business. Try issuing a press release every month, following the guidelines in the press relations and press lists chapters and using the press release templates. If it does work, keep up the monthly momentum.

Basically, when you are drawing up your PR plan, think about a range of activities to deliver key messages to your chosen audience.

Try and select a PR activity from each of the following main groups:

1. **Information provision:** where you are the direct source and provider of information. It is under your complete control. This is likely to mean that you are paying to produce the information material yourself. This is the most expensive PR option, although it can be the least time-consuming.

2. **Press relations:** where you are the indirect source of the information and someone else is paying to produce the material. It is not under your control, but it is more powerful because the information is in the form of an expert recommendation from the editorial staff.
3. **General PR and communications techniques:** mainly aimed at improving the status and prestige of the organisation among a select audience. These PR techniques usually involve some expense, but generally give great value for money.

Developing the PR plan

List your resources, selected PR techniques, key messages and your target audience. Work out a plan of action that includes at least one PR activity each month.

Think about what you want to achieve.

Perhaps you want to boost business at a local level? In which case an 'open day' for customers and potential customers, or corporate hospitality for key customers might do a lot for your business.

You can, of course, get the best of both worlds since all these activities can be good excuses to send out press releases.

It's quite easy to be carried away with the demands of the media, to the extent that you could end up generating more demand than you can fulfil. Clearly that is going to lead to disappointment and ultimately detract from your reputation. That is why we have devised a PR questionnaire to help define your PR goals.

Implementing the PR plan

The questionnaire should help you determine what you want to achieve with PR. It is designed to help you focus on the type of potential customers and audience you want to reach, the press coverage you want to generate and your measures of success. You will have also defined the resources you have to achieve your PR goals.

PR works best when you can plan a steady stream of press releases and events: perhaps one a month, or one every second month. It sometimes takes two or three press releases before journalists really believe you are serious. The more publicity you get, the easier it is to get more. So if at first you don't succeed, don't give up. You are already a few steps further down the road than you were at the start.

When you have finished reading this book, plan a year of projected PR activity, with something every month or so: press releases, letters offering to address key audiences, hospitality and events.

American banks now look for a PR plan as part of the business plan. Why wait to be asked? Add your PR plan as a chapter in your business plan.

The PR Questionnaire

I.   Goals

What are your overall business objectives for the next financial year?

- Consolidation or expansion
- Projected sales figures
- Projected profit
- Projected turnover
- Projected staff
- Projected new products or services
- New markets
- Existing markets
- Other goals?

Which goal is the most important success indicator for your business?

What target will you use to judge that success? For example: what percentage increase in profits=success? Or percentage increase in market share?

Where do you want to be in five years?

Do your answers to the questions above reflect these five-year goals?

2. SWOT Analysis
(Strengths, Weaknesses, Opportunities, Threats)

Threats

- What are the greatest challenges for your business in the year ahead?
- What stands between you and success?
- Who are your main competitors?

Opportunities
What are your key PR opportunities?

- Have you got new products or services in the pipeline?
- Who are the people you need to reach to maximise these opportunities?
- Do you have access to facts and figures for sales material and press releases?
- Are you planning events or activities that might generate press coverage?
- Can you divide potential customers into categories: size? industrial sector? geographical area?
- What are potential clients' opinions of your company and its products/services?
- In your opinion, who influences your customers?

Strengths

- Do you have connections with any trade, business or professional bodies/associations?
- Do you have any champion customers who would endorse your products or services?

- Are you comfortable about being interviewed by members of the press?
- Do you have business partners or key staff who are good communicators?

Weaknesses

- If your business had a higher profile, would there be problems to address?
- In the last five years, have you had any bad press reports about you or your business?
- Do you have any disgruntled customers who would create problems if you adopted a higher profile?
- Do you have any disaffected staff or former business associates?

3. PR Focus

How do you see PR helping you achieve your business goals during the next financial year?

- What targets will have to be met to judge your PR efforts a success?
- If you could only do two PR things in the next year, what would they be?
- How much money can you put aside for the year's PR activities?
- Do you think this budget will allow you to achieve your stated PR goals?
- How much time can you devote to PR in the forthcoming year?
- Which press do you really want to get into?

©Penny Haywood PR 1998

PR techniques symbols

🕐   time consuming

£/$ moderate costs involved (over and above basic expenses)

££/$$ heavier costs involved

📖   needs good contacts database

🎧   can lead to a high public profile

💾   a computer would be helpful

🗐   lots of paperwork involved

🖅   lots of postage or faxing involved

☎   lots of telephoning involved

❝❞   good press coverage potential

✷   prestigious

⊙   good for reaching tightly targeted groups of people

☺   boosts sales

Most symbols are self-explanatory. Some need further clarification.

Where both money symbols appear: **£/$ ££/$$** , it means there's money involved; but you should be able to find moderate as well as more expensive options.

The difference between 🎧 (high profile) and ✷ (prestigious) is that a high profile will get you known to a mass audience, whereas prestige-raising activities may be limited to a more select audience. Providing this select audience includes key potential clients, it may be considerably less time-consuming and more profitable to opt for ✷ prestige than to go for the 🎧 high profile in a mass market. If, however, you need a high public profile to shift large numbers of goods to lots of different people, ✷ prestige will not figure as strongly as a 🎧 high public profile.

📖 Means you need a good contacts database: generally 3,000 entries or more for a flourishing small business. The database will be a mixture of potential clients, support people and suppliers. To that mix, you will also add press lists and contacts. It does not matter whether you hold the records on computer, in address books or on a card index. (NB You will have to comply with data protection legislation if you hold details on a computer.) It will be much easier to update and manipulate the database, produce mail-merged letters to key people, and generate mailing labels if the data is on computer. Some people manage by photocopying lists onto labels for mass postal distribution.

☺ This symbol denotes activities that are likely to directly lead to sales opportunities, sales referrals, sales enquiries and sales leads.

PR and communications techniques checklist

1.   Information provision

Advertisements	🕐	££/$$	🎧		☉☺
Brochures	🕐	££/$$			★☉☺
Exhibitions	🕐	££/$$		" "	☉☺
Financial information					★☉
Leaflets and flyers	🕐 £/$ ££/$$		🎧		☉☺
Newsletters	🕐 £/$ ££/$$ 📖🎧💾📄✉				★☉☺
Open days	🕐 £/$			" "	☉
Presentations	🕐				☉☺
Public meetings	🕐	📖🎧		" "	
Roadshows	🕐	££/$$		" "	☉☺
Seminars	🕐 £/$ ££/$$ 📖		✉☎ " "		★☉☺
Video	🕐	££/$$			★☉☺
Websites	🕐 £/$				☉☺

2.   Press

Press relations	🕐	📖🎧💾📄✉☎ " " ★	☺

3.   PR and general communications

Ambassadors	🕐	📖		★☉☺
Awards	🕐 £/$ ££/$$		" "	★☉
Charities	🕐	🎧	" "	★☉
Contacts database	🕐	📖 💾📄✉☎		☉☺
Corporate hospitality	🕐 £/$ ££/$$			★☉☺
Design	🕐 £/$ ££/$$			★
Events	🕐 £/$ ££/$$ 📖		" "	★☉
Lobbying	🕐	📖🎧💾📄✉☎ " "		★☉
Networking	🕐	📖		☉☺
Sponsorship	🕐 £/$ ££/$$		" "	★☉ ☺
Staff relations	🕐			☺

©Penny Haywood PR 1998

Techniques by results chart

Desired results	Most effective techniques (in alphabetical order)
High public profile	Advertisements
	Charities
	Leaflets and flyers
	Lobbying (if appropriate)
	Newsletters
	Press relations
	Public meetings (if appropriate)
More contacts	Ambassadors
	Contacts database
	Events
	Networking
	Roadshows
	Seminars
	Sponsorship
More prestige	Ambassadors
	Awards
	Brochures
	Charities
	Corporate hospitality
	Design
	Events
	Financial information
	Lobbying (if appropriate)
	Newsletters
	Press relations
	Public meetings (if appropriate)
	Seminars
	Sponsorship
	Video

Reaching a targeted audience

Advertisements
Ambassadors
Awards
Brochures
Charities
Contacts database
Corporate hospitality
Events
Exhibitions
Financial information
Leaflets and flyers
Lobbying (if appropriate)
Networking
Newsletters
Open days
Presentations
Press relations (specific trade press)
Roadshows
Seminars
Sponsorship

Sales boost

Advertisements
Ambassadors
Brochures
Contacts database
Corporate hospitality
Exhibitions
Leaflets and flyers
Networking
Newsletters
Presentations
Press relations
Roadshows
Seminars
Video
Websites

PR techniques and restricted resources

Limited resource	PR technique
Low money?	*Concentrate on*
	Ambassadors
	Charities
	Contacts database
	Financial information
	Lobbying (if appropriate)
	Networking
	Press relations
	Presentations
	Staff relations
	Public meetings (if appropriate)
A little money?	*As above, plus*
	Awards
	Corporate hospitality
	Design
	Events
	Leaflets and flyers
	Newsletters
	Open days
	Seminars
	Sponsorships in kind
	Website

Few contacts?	*Concentrate on*
	Ambassadors
	Awards
	Contacts database
	Networking
	Open days
	Press relations
	Sponsorships
	Website
No computer?	*Consider*
	Advertisements
	Ambassadors
	Awards
	Corporate hospitality
	Design
	Events
	Exhibitions
	Leaflets/brochures
	Networking
	Open days
	Presentations
	Roadshows
	Press relations (local and key trade press)
	Seminars
	Sponsorship
	Staff relations
	Video
No time?	Advertise or re-examine your priorities to make time for PR

©Penny Haywood PR 1998

CHAPTER 3:

THE MARKETING PLAN

It's no good making a great product or delivering the best service in the world if people don't know about it, or if they think there is a problem associated with it.

At first, many small businesses trade off existing connections: word-of-mouth recommendation from friends and former colleagues. That word-of-mouth recommendation is the strongest form of advertising you can get. But few people are lucky enough to be able to form a life-long business on personal contacts alone.

That means reaching a wider public by publicising the business and information about its products.

It takes time and energy to develop new products or ideas and find the markets for them. But without a marketing plan you are going off in all directions, losing the chance to identify and develop your most profitable areas of business.

Your marketing plan will bring all your promotional activity together and provide a business framework for your PR goals.

It has been said that you need to spend as much as half your time marketing to reach your full potential share of your target market. You have to market to stand still: it's estimated that businesses lose 10% of their business on average each year through no fault of their own. Buyers move on, clients collapse, new brooms have favoured suppliers, or customers' needs change and your products or services are left behind.

What is a marketing plan?

Most people think *marketing* is *advertising* or *market research* or a fancy word for selling. All these answers are partly right. The purpose of marketing is to detail how you are going to turn products and services into cash. Marketing is the art of getting the right product or service to the right people at the right price. Sounds easy enough, but how do you find out whether you have a product or service that is right for people to buy? What is the right price? How do you make sure it finds its way to the right people?

The answer is that you start with market research, then build up a plan to handle pricing, distribution and promotion.

If PR takes care of the bigger picture, the reputation of the company, marketing takes care of individual products and services. That is why businesses need to address each product/service or range separately within their marketing plans. Let us go through the marketing plan step by step.

I.   Research

The first step is to research what you are marketing and who the customer is. A shortcut to success is to know more than your competition about your markets. In that way, you can choose which messages will be more effective for each group you want to target.

- Research the overall size of your potential market as well as individual needs and wants of customers.
- Research who your competition is, why people buy from them, and uncover the external factors that influence your market, such as the economy or legislation.

According to Barclays Bank, the failure to conduct initial research is probably a contributory factor in the high failure rate of new businesses. One-fifth of UK businesses close within twelve months of starting up. An incredible seven out of ten UK entrepreneurs set up without carrying out any research to determine if a market for their business exists.

It's not just business start-ups who neglect research. If you have been in business for a while, could you be getting complacent? It's all too easy to think you know who your customers are and what they want, so you don't bother to ask any more.

Make sure you are not offering an average service. Ask for suggestions for ways you could help your customers even more.

Real information comes from real customers. If you are selling high value products or services, forget fancy questionnaires; ring them up, or take them out to lunch and talk to them. This will not only provide valuable insight into the current customers' needs and satisfaction levels regarding price, packaging, service etc. It could also encourage referrals.

Your research may uncover complaints. Don't despair: complaints are golden opportunities. Customers understand that not everything or everyone works perfectly all the time. What distinguishes the men from the boys is how well you cope with the inevitable glitches. If you handle it well, you increase customer loyalty significantly.

A short questionnaire (five questions maximum, with tick boxes for answers) on the table would be fine for a restaurant, wine bar, coffee house or any other business where customers are seated with time on their hands. Encourage interest by entering respondents in a monthly prize draw if they give their name and telephone number.

Talk to ex-customers when they cancel an order or you notice they haven't come back. Ring them up without any pressure and see whether there was a better offer somewhere else, or a problem with your customer service. You will never know if you don't ask.

- Establish the market for your product or service by looking at your competitors
- Draw up a customer profile to understand your prospective clients' buying habits
- Monitor the market regularly for changing conditions and new opportunities.

2.   Define the goals

Some companies need to gain just one new customer in a specialised field per year. Others may only need 30 new clients in a clearly-defined sector to achieve their goals. In this case, using PR as a sales support to generate blanket press coverage reaching hundreds of thousands of people is clearly a waste of time when you can focus down so clearly. You may want to carry out some specialised press relations activity to boost your reputation; that is a PR rather than a marketing issue.

Marketing plans should ideally contain business goals for one, three and five years, to focus on the short, medium and longer term. The plan should identify key cut-off dates for reaching goals. Progress should be reviewed regularly.

The marketing plan is centred on your Unique Selling Proposition (USP): the reason someone will choose to buy your product or service rather than that of your competitors. Then you have to decide how best to communicate your USP to the marketplace.

3. The 5 Ps

The famous 5 Ps of marketing a product or service have to be addressed in a marketing plan. They are:

- **Product** (or service) and its USP
- **Packaging:** how it will be presented to the potential buyer
- **Promotion:** the methods you will choose to get sales messages across
- **Price:** in comparison to the competition, your costs (including a proportion of overheads) and the margin of profit you expect
- **Place:** which means how you get it to the customer – distribution

Which of the 5 Ps is most important to marketing your product or service? Second most important? And so on. Getting the mix of the 5 Ps right will determine a successful marketing plan.

You may decide you will not be beaten on price, so that becomes your most important marketing tool.

You may decide that packaging or presentation is all-important.

If you chose to rely on promotion, make sure you have variety in your promotional activity. Over-reliance on word-of-mouth for developing new business restricts your potential client base. The Chartered Institute of Marketing advises "Use a carefully targeted mixture of advertising, public relations and focused direct mailings to help broaden your customer base".

There are more promotional tools than any business could afford. Which will work best for you? All businesses are different and what works for one may be a dud for another. Here's a list of the most common, together with their main pros and cons.

THE MARKETING PLAN

- **Advertising**
  - ✔ Good for getting quick results for certain types of business
  - ✗ The cost.

- **Brochures**
  - ✔ Good for illustrating products but expensive to do well.
  - ✗ Not good for low budgets as they start going out of date from the moment they are printed. Consider a folder instead, so that you can insert loose pages; or a website where information can be easily updated.

- **Database development** and selective telephone calls or mailings with follow up calls to arrange a meeting.
  - ✔ Good for higher value sales, business-to-business sales and for generating one-to-one sales opportunities.
  - ✗ Not so good for retail outlets or low value sales.

- **Direct response mail**
  - ✔ Good for generating high awareness.
  - ✗ Not good for budgets as attractive mailshots can be quite expensive.

- **Exhibitions and fairs**
  - ✔ Good for people with unusually visual products or very good graphics. It's better if you are invited to share exhibition space; some trade and enterprise organisations will let you use part of their stand without charge.
  - ✗ Not so good for businesses with low budgets or low impact visuals. Often expensive and very easy to be swamped by everyone else. Have a good prize draw at your stand to collect names and addresses of visitors and liaise with the organisers' press office if you are announcing a new product or service during the event.

■ **Internet**

✔ Relatively inexpensive to set up but needs to be imaginative and regularly changed to keep them coming back. Needs to be backed up with advertising and effort to encourage visitors to the site.

✘ Not good for businesses with customers who are not into the net.

■ **Lead generation programmes**

Campaigns where you encourage customers to recommend friends.

✔ Good for businesses that rely on critical purchases, where people have to buy if they have a need (virtually any form of repair service is in this category). Once you have got the lead, make sure you follow up with literature or a call, maybe offering a special customers' 24 hour 'hotline' or a first time users' free offer.

✘ Not so good for professional expertise providers where it can look a bit desperate; try networking instead.

■ **Networking**

✔ One of the best ways for 'expert' service providers to reach a wider audience. Keep practising key messages and attend various groups several times to achieve best results.

✘ Not good for people who are shy or short of time.

■ **Newsletters**

✔ Good for businesses with services and expertise to demonstrate in case studies. Allows you to put your name in front of customers and potential customers. This keeps them up to date on a regular basis for less cost than a brochure.

✘ Not good for very low budgets or very small target audiences.

■ **Presentations**
  ✔ Good for expertise-based businesses.
  ✗ Not good for people who dislike standing up in front of an audience.

■ **Public relations press coverage**
  ✔ Good for raising reputation and profile, generating mass awareness and establishing expertise. And good for creating the sort of ambience where sales are easier to make.
  ✗ Not good for people with little time to look after the press or businesses with few new services or products.

■ **Seminars** can offer a free taster of your expertise.
  ✔ Good for any business that sells expertise.
  ✗ Not good for people who hate public speaking and presentations.

Sometimes your marketing research can be the most effective sales tool. Telephone marketing can identify and survey key decision makers in target companies and assess their willingness to consider the company's product. Don't put them off with a sales pitch in the same telephone call. No-one likes to feel they have been duped. Giving you time to help define their needs for market research is one thing: sales presentations are another.

Every business and its targeted audience are different. Sometimes every product is for a different market. But whatever you do, once you have got the marketing plan(s), use them.

4. Keep tracking

Make sure you keep watching how you are doing and assessing what works and what does not. Note what you got against what it cost and the time it took. Some marketing ploys work better than others, so log results and learn from them. Sales levels are an obvious indicator. But for an in-depth view, customer questionnaires and focus groups will improve your understanding of customers' needs, as well as broadening and updating your customer database.

Don't expect miracles overnight. A common mistake made by small businesses is to give up on marketing too early. If you have taken on too much work, cut the plan back to more realistic levels or delegate some of the routine work.

Review every three to six months unless you are in a fast-changing manufacturing business. In this case you will need monthly reviews.

5.   Keep an eye on the competition

What do they do right? What could they do better? If possible, buy from them. Ring up to find out what they are like to deal with and how they handle enquiries.

6.   Budget

What budget? This is a book about free publicity, isn't it? Yes, but if you are already in business, you are already spending time and money on marketing, even if you don't call it that.

Research for the organisers of the Business Solutions show in London found that smaller companies spend over 600% more on sales and marketing than they spend on their next largest annual spend: information technology.

The survey showed that 85.7% already have, or plan to invest in, a corporate brochure over the next 12 months; 62.8% in advertising; and

55% in sales promotion. Some 62.1% plan to launch new products or services over the next 12 months.

The survey revealed that 38.6% of the small businesses surveyed are currently logged on to the Internet, with 88.9% using it for advertising, marketing or sales. The figures for the US will be higher because take-up of the Internet is ahead of the UK.

Even if you have not formally earmarked money for marketing, you will have probably spent something on visiting, or writing to, potential customers. Maybe you have taken an ad hoc advertisement in a trade directory, *Yellow Pages* or a bold entry in the phone book? Have you phoned potential customers? Spent money on display materials? Taken customers out to lunch? Exhibited at a fair? Had leaflets printed? It's all too easy to run away with four-figure sums in small bits, without planning your marketing spend.

Many small businesses spend money promoting their business on an ad hoc basis. To convert that into a budget, work out how much you spent last year and use that figure as a base. There is no faster or more effective way to get rid of persistent advertising salespeople than to tell them you are sorry, but you have overspent your advertising budget for this year. They hear it all the time from larger businesses and experience has taught them it's fruitless to persist.

7. Explore profitability

There are only three ways to boost business profitability:

- Increase existing sales revenue
- Spend less money
- Find new customers

Most businesses raise prices when they need more cash. But modifying all three tactics by a small percentage makes a bigger cumulative difference and upsets customers less.

Finding new customers is much more expensive than generating more sales from existing customers. So whether you have a corner shop or management consultancy, a manufacturing business or leisure industry, the first priority is to find ways to tempt existing customers to spend more or more often. If you are selling business-to-business, the more people and departments you sell to within a major corporation, the better chance you have of keeping that prestigious name on your list of clients.

Spending less money is not only about cutting back on budgets and spending commitments, it's looking at how you apportion expenditure in the first place. Are you distributing a fair share of overheads across your product or service range? Are some taking longer to service than others? If so, profitability should reflect the cost of that extra time. If you don't, and that time-consuming product takes off as a result of good PR and marketing, how would you cope? What would happen to your profits? Could you keep up quality and customer service? If not, you are in deep trouble. Concentrate on developing the ranges or markets that are really profitable.

8. Plan for growth

Too much growth? You wish! But it's a dream that can quickly turn into a nightmare. Press relations in particular can be a very powerful tool; you have to be careful it's not too effective.

We once generated sales of £60 million (c$100 million) of financial investment 'product' in just three months, mainly through press relations. The client coped with a doubling of staff (from 12-25) within a few months of that success. They spent weeks in near-chaos, with workmen all around them, as premises were adapted and extended to cope with the influx.

The accelerating demands of a fast-growth situation can lead to a full scale clash between staff, finance and production capabilities. As any banker knows, business expansion is fraught with danger. That is why they can be singularly unhelpful when you are flushed with success.

The reason? Any dramatic sales increase puts pressure on customer service, delivery times or quality, touching off a downward spiral of cancelled orders and over-production that can only end in tears.

That is why you need to build in flexibility to your stated delivery dates: you can always exceed expectations but you do need to give yourself room to manoeuvre when business is booming.

Success, like deadlines, has a habit of sneaking up on you. Small business owners are used to solving problems themselves. It can be hard to come to terms with the prospect of limiting the business to what you can do in a day. It's all too easy to delay getting other people in to manage the effects of growth until it's too late.

A plan for growth has to involve increased delegation. It's better to be responsible for 50 per cent of something that is five times bigger than looking after 100 per cent of a smaller business. Even planned growth has its chaotic phases, so build in incentives that reward staff for going the extra mile when things get rough. Get used to be continually communicating, explaining to people what their contributions are and managing their day-to-day expectations.

Because banks have a habit of dragging their feet on expansion, you need clear evidence that you have forecast this growth and planned for it. Before you implement the techniques in this book, take the time to discuss your growth plan with the bank manger. See if he thinks there are obvious gaps in your preparation.

Painful as it sounds, in times of rapid growth you may have to focus only on the most promising opportunities. That is why it's important to have an accurate knowledge of the profitability of all your sales lines. It makes more sense for small businesses to focus on core competencies and their current customer base, than to shoot off in all directions. It's all too easy to become fixated by the short-term gains of chasing the sale. You end up being not very good in several markets rather than developing depth and strength. Having said that, there is security in diversity if you have enough people to handle it.

Don't forget to keep your family aware of this pressure when you are handling growth. You are likely to be ignoring friends and family and that will catch up with you in time. The last thing you want are personal problems when you are at your busiest. You need to be able to get away from the business for a long weekend once in a while to keep fresh and strengthen bonds with the people around you.

9. Brush up your selling skills

Usually the opposite of growth is the problem for small businesses. Because they often rely on personal contacts during the initial stages, businesses are carried along on a network of friends and acquaintances. But sooner or later, you will have to expand your horizons if you want to grow. A marketing plan that includes sales training and personal development skills for yourself and key staff is realistic if you are not in that line of business already.

Sadly, old fashioned sales stereotypes still persist in small businesses, and they often come on far too strong and turn people off. People make buying decisions on emotion, then justify it later with reasoning. Successful selling is guiding people to make buying decisions then convincing them they have, taking all the factors into account, made the best value for money choice.

10. Customers give you the edge

For competitive edge, keep focused on customer service and commitment to quality.

Even if your product or service is better, you have to accept that sales success is 50% product or service-based and 50% public relations. That is why good products lose out to marginally worse products if the reputation of the other company is better.

Make sure you have a customer care section in the marketing plan, with a well-tested plan of action for complaints, together with target deadlines for each stage in dealing with the problem. Set a deadline for updating the customer and assure them you are going flat out to solve the problem. Of course, every business is different; in a restaurant, or on a computer advice hotline, your action has to be prompt. A management consultant may be dealing with something much more complex and a longer deadline may be more acceptable.

A complaint well-handled often turns an irate person into a strong advocate for your business. Strangely enough, the most irate person often turns into your most powerful ally because they care deeply about the product or service.

11. Advertising

Most business books and courses teach start-up businesses how to research their basic business idea to ensure there is a market for the product or service, then advise advertising.

There is nothing wrong with advertising except the cost, which can be far too high for small businesses. But if you are going to ditch advertising altogether, you have to have a strong marketing plan with varied promotional activities.

Few advertising salespeople will tell you that it takes about three inserts before readers even notice an advertisement is there – and that is for quite a large display ad. Just think about the last newspaper you read. How many adverts can you remember? I bet it's not many, unless a competitor had a big spread. You glossed over whole-page adverts costing more than you will probably budget for a year's marketing spend.

As for classified ads, they are not suitable for many products or services. Who would choose a business adviser from a small ad nestling between the escort agencies, the personal column and household wares? However, if you run an escort agency or want to offload lots of beds fast, the classifieds are probably one of your first marketing choices.

If you are tempted to advertise, profit from your competitors' experience. If they are advertising heavily and repeatedly in something, they are either mad or it works. There are times to be a pioneer in business but advertising is not usually one of them, especially when you are a small business.

Never pay to be a guinea pig to see whether an advertising medium will work for your business sector. The chances are plenty of companies have paid the price in the past.

New publications, especially directories, are notorious. They will offer huge discounts, often on very impressive-looking sales forms but few survive long enough to establish themselves. Those that do may work for some types of businesses and not for others. There is no point in backing someone else's unproved business venture when you have got your own business to look after.

12. PR as sales support

Check out press release ideas and other low cost PR techniques in this book before shelling out to market you business.

CHAPTER 4

PR TECHNIQUES

The following is a mix of PR and related communication techniques. Many are 'free' in that they are designed to take your key business messages to a larger audience. The 'costs' involved are your time, your powers of persuasion, post, fax or phone.

Other PR techniques, such as *Awards,* involve a small outlay for a suitable trophy or prize. However, they are designed to return benefits well in excess of the equivalent amount spent on advertising.

Techniques like *Design* are not free. They have to be included in a PR plan because, to be credible, your business image needs to be in step with the reputation you use PR to create.

To help you decide what would work best for your PR plan, the following symbols have been used. Decide what's most important to you, and what resources you can realistically devote to PR, then let the symbols guide you to the possible PR techniques to achieve your business goals.

○	time consuming
£/$	moderate costs involved (over and above basic expenses)
££/$$	heavier costs involved
▥	needs good contacts database
♀	can lead to a high public profile

PR TECHNIQUES

    💾   a computer would be helpful

    📄   lots of paperwork involved

    🖹   lots of postage or faxing involved

    ☎   lots of telephoning involved

    ❝❞   good press coverage potential

    ★   prestigious

    ☉   good for reaching tightly targeted groups of people

    ☺   boosts sales

Advertisements

🕒 ££/$$ 🎧 ☉ ☺

When you need specific fast results and you have little or no news content to offer. Special offers, staff recruitment, etc.

Virtually all quoted advertising rates can be reduced by a third. So haggle, explore regional edition options, and haggle again. If you anticipate advertising more than once a year, try for a group discount. See page 84 for more details on advertising, advertorials and editorial.

Ambassadors

 ★ ☉ ☺

These are prominent individuals from business, industry, commerce, professional bodies, societies, associations or universities, local councils and governing bodies who, through their relevant position and experience, are able to make influential recommendations. They may be customers, old colleagues, friends, fellow committee members in professional bodies or contacts from the past. Seek to develop ambassador relationships so that you can quote their positive remarks to promote your business. List ambassadors on your PR plan. Ambassadors lend a great deal of credibility to your organisation. They will actively promote your business, while 'opinion-formers' (q.v.) are more remote. You will seek to influence opinion-formers, but it's unlikely that an opinion-former will actively promote your business in the way an ambassador does.

Awards

🕓 £/$ ££/$$ 66 99 ✴ ⊙

Awards are excellent if you are aiming at a highly-targeted group. They can be used to bring your name to the attention of professional and trade organisations and potential customers. With a little creativity, you can use awards to solve a variety of problems.

Awards case study:
The recruiting ploy

Small businesses lose out in recruiting graduates because larger companies have sophisticated recruitment techniques to pick off the cream. The answer? Contact the local university or college that is best at offering courses in the subjects you want and ask whether they would like an award for their students, possibly coupled with some work experience. Responses will vary, but the more switched-on educationalists will just about bite your hand off for such an opportunity.

Offer to meet with the head of the appropriate department to discuss their needs. The best offer is a trophy to show you are in there for the longer term, plus a cash award for the financially-challenged student, plus a short work experience opportunity which lecturers often find difficult to arrange. Choose to give the award for an outstanding class project in something related to your field so you can identify the most promising students before they commit themselves to someone else.

Try and build up a rapport with the lecturers and, if possible, show you are open to offering work experience places. In the long term, you will be in a position to get one of the first choices of students and a chance to try them out. Even if the work trial isn't what that particular student wants, they will know others who might well be interested. The students you meet, and some of the lecturers, will be able to recommend students who are still looking for a job. Small companies may not have the kudos of a large corporate but they can offer more freedom and challenges.

Awards case study:
The rare expertise

A participant at one of my DIYPR workshops said at the end: "Well, PR's no good for me. Only six companies in the world can use my services".

I didn't believe him at first, but it was true. He had a very obscure speciality, but he was one of the best in his field. He had the most tightly-defined market I have ever encountered and his problem was raising awareness of his expertise among the few people that would hire his consultancy. He did agree that placing articles demonstrating his expertise in the few relevant trade publications would enhance his reputation.

Another option would be to create an award of excellence in

conjunction with a relevant professional body. Invite the key sales targets to be on the judging panel that he, as the award founder, would chair.

Not all will accept, but his name has gone in front of his key targets in a prestigious capacity, and he'll send out a report to the specialist press. He'd make sure that his career highlights (maximum 100 words) were included with papers showing aims of the award and judging criteria, distributed to all potential judges.

If no-one accepts, he's still got his expertise in front of the key audience and a subsequent sales call can refer to the awards material. If any do accept the judging invitation, then, bingo! He's won up to a whole day closeted with the very people he's been trying to reach, in a strong position to quietly demonstrate his expertise.

As long as he does not show his sales hand during the awards process, he'll be able to send a helpful follow-up letter after the judging and start to build up a long-term relationship without pressure. A comment is all it takes to give an excuse to write or call. "I remembered what you said about ... and thought you'd be interested in the enclosed..." If he was too obvious about his motives during the awards, he'd risk bringing the whole award, and his reputation, into disrepute.

Patience is the key to building up long-term high value sales, such as consultancy. In the PR business it can take from six months to three years to build up a business relationship: a time span that I am sure will be familiar to many other business consultants.

Brochures

🕐 ££/$$ ★☉☺

There comes a time when most businessmen's thoughts turn to producing a brochure. Usually it's when the business owner comes across a competitors' particularly impressive publication. However, the chances are that the intended recipients will take one look and wonder how much of their fees are going towards fancy brochures.

Brochures are expensive sops to the business owner's ego. No-one wants to wade through chunks of flagrant sales copy and it all starts going out of date from the moment it's printed.

Developing a website may be a cheaper alternative if most of your clients have Internet access, and it's not expensive to keep up-to-date.

If you really feel you must leave something decent sitting on prospective clients' desks, consider a customised pre-printed folder to take loose leaf inserts which you can have printed as you need them. That way, you can select sheets giving product or service details, case histories, customer endorsements, client and price lists, to suit the client. Effectively, every folder becomes a bespoke brochure.

Charities

🕐 🎧 ❝❞ ★☉

Linking up with a charity is a good way to put something back into the community and it is by no means a one-way benefit. Charities often have a high profile, with high profile patrons and board members. Reputable charities have the ability to confer a tremendous amount of associated goodwill onto a business.

'The chairman's whim' used to be the joke in PR circles for the way larger businesses became involved with charities. While a certain amount of personal enthusiasm is necessary to ensure your involvement is credible, there's no reason why you can't take a focused approach to charitable involvement. For example, is someone you want to influence involved in a charity? Is there an industry-related charity allied to your business sector that would give you good contacts?

Decide whether it would be more appropriate to be involved with a local or national charity. Have a look in the *Yellow Pages* to get an idea of which organisations are represented in your area.

Once you start working with a charity, you will be approached by others, so have a clear cut budget and policy, perhaps focusing on themes such as *youth, sport, disability, cancer research etc.*

Being involved with a charity in your own area of expertise may provide interesting opportunities to meet influential people and allow you to contribute in kind rather than cash. For example, an optician might be involved in collecting unwanted glasses destined for under-developed countries. He might sit on the board of a charity for the partially-sighted. Both the board appointment and the 'old specs' collection campaign would be subjects for a press release.

Fund-raising events are another good way to generate publicity for the charity and yourself. You can often be much more creative with events done for charity, so make sure that livewires are pulled into a 'publicity think tank', to generate photo opportunities and publicity ideas.

The *Guinness Book of Records* could inspire some highly-photogenic world record attempts, with participants heavily sponsored of course.

Contacts databases

Not so much a PR technique as an invaluable PR and marketing resource. Love your database and care for it: it's the engine of your business, particularly if you don't have a retail outlet.

PR TECHNIQUES

There's nothing worse than mis-spelling someone's name or getting their job title wrong. Whether it's in an address book, on record cards or on the latest computer, mailing lists have to be maintained meticulously. Record the date you update a record in an update column or field.

While direct mail is more properly a marketing than PR tool, there is no reason why you cannot send news releases based on press releases to potential customers, or include news releases with the rest of your mailshot material.

While we are on the subject of mailshots, the trick is to develop the knack of saying what the customer wants to hear, not what you want to tell them. It sounds simple enough, but many people find it hard to throw away well-loved product description detail. For example, the latest modem with blistering bps figures, PC-compatibility and other technical guff translates in terms of customer benefits as: "The fastest way to surf the net". The detail can be mopped up in the small print.

Don't expect too much from a mailshot: it's a numbers game. Response rates of 0.5-2.0% are not uncommon. Well-targeted mailing lists and good sales copy could take you to 5 or 6%. You have still got to convert enquiries into sales...

Enclosures increase response rates, whether it's a tea-bag or sachet of coffee: "have a cuppa while you consider our offer" to a giant paper clip or a free product sample. The more innovative, the more memorable, as long as it's reasonably appropriate to your business.

I've met managers of new businesses who think they've got a terrific database with 150 entries and they may well have if they are all potential buyers of a high value service. I've also met small businesses who were apologetic about having only 5,000 contacts.

It's hard to generalise but, as a rule, I feel more comfortable when small business clients selling a fairly high value service have at least 3-5,000 fairly recent names in the database. That is to support 1-3 staff. More mouths to feed will mean more potential names.

A fast way to get more names for the database is through on-line searches, although searches are not usually free of charge. CompuServe has a relatively low-cost business information service that will suit many small business users.

Dun & Bradstreet offers on-line company listings containing the name, address and contact information, plus a summary, financial data, parent and subsidiary information and key directors. You can access D&B's web-based direct marketing service, enabling you to make up your own targeted mailing list. You can specify selection criteria such as type of business, turnover, geographical location and number of employees. An initial search is free. The reports can be sent by e-mail, fax or post. Find out more on Dun & Bradstreet's website at http://www.dunandbrad.co.uk.

If you are lucky enough to have a business library in your area, check out their CD-ROM business databases. The City Business Library in London and National Library of Scotland have excellent business research facilities. Most Chambers of Commerce have good directories and some are equipped with CD-ROM or on-line facilities. TECs and LECs are another potential source of business information. (See the sources appendix for contact information.)

The alternative is to keep an eye on appointments columns in magazines and newspapers. Many newly-promoted people sweep out old suppliers to put their own stamp on a job; it's a good idea to write within the first two weeks of a new appointment.

Corporate Hospitality

🕐 £/$ ££/$$ ✱ ⊙ ☺

Surely you don't need advice on how to entertain people? Well, a lot can go wrong with something that starts out looking very simple. The key to making a good impression is professional planning and preparation.

Rule 1: Check it out. Whether it's a seminar or meeting, or just a meal, make sure you know if your guests have any special dietary requirements. Taking a vegetarian to a steakhouse will not do much for your order book. Confirm bookings for premises, equipment and special requirements in writing or fax. Always arrive in time to check the premises and test any equipment you may be using.

Even something as straightforward as taking someone out to lunch needs preparation if you have not been to that restaurant before. Pop in early and make sure the waiters know you are a host with an important guest. Have a look at the menu and discuss anything you are not sure of so that you, in turn, will be able to enlighten your guest instead of having to call the waiter over. Find out where cloakrooms are and check whether service is included on the bill. Well-run establishments will appreciate an attention to detail that mirrors their own. They may well greet you like one of their best customers when you return later with your guest. At the very least, you will be confident and comfortable with the arrangements.

Rule 2: Look after them. Make sure special diets are properly catered for. Don't leave people stranded. Make sure there's a welcome for them at the door, so they are not left to find their own way to a room in a hotel that is running six other events that day. Think about your guest's convenience and arrange transport from a late function, especially if alcohol is involved. Feed and water guests if you keep them over a mealtime or teabreak.

Rule 3: Give them a reminder. If you have spent time and money getting to know someone, don't send them away empty-handed. Try and prolong the effect with a reminder of your business: a business card at least, or a leaflet. In some circumstances a small gift works well: a pen with your company name or a small sample of your product, if appropriate. A personal touch can work well. Several clients framed a limited edition hand-printed Christmas card we produced last year. If you are into innovative gifts, make sure they can't backfire. Drinks mats made from computer disks, easily confused with ordinary disks, were binned very quickly in our office.

Design
🕐 £/$ ££/$$ ✶

If you have a well-established corporate identity, think twice about doing anything more than modernising it. Shell and BP, for example, spend millions on 'tweaking' their logos every few years to keep them up to date. They don't throw the whole thing away because they know it takes years of effort to establish a new corporate identity.

Why is corporate identity so important?

Psychologists tell us that we naturally tend to group images or patterns. We are all subjected to hundreds of logos every day: on TV, in publications, on the bus or tube and in the mail. Once we see a logo three or four times, we begin to recognise it. The more we see it the more familiar it becomes, and that familiarity brings with it an important benefit.

The more familiar a logo is, the more we trust it, and trust is an important part of business reputation. That is why a consistent corporate identity is important to the PR plan.

However, if you are not happy with your corporate image, try to budget for professional help to give it a lift. The better the brief, the better the results, so think about the words you use to describe your business. Collect examples of logos, business cards or letterheads that you like, competitors' brochures and literature that you admire and think would be an appropriate style.

Think about the colours that suit your business. Neutrals are a bit dull. Blues appeal to men and are quite cool and professional. Greens gives off environmentally friendly signals. Yellow is difficult to see on a white background. Reds, pinks and oranges appeal to women and are warm and impulsive colours. Pastels are insipid for most businesses. Fashion comes into this. It's no sin to be influenced by fashion, provided you have a history of liking the colour anyway and feel it's reasonably appropriate for the business.

For example: a wild and wacky logo indicating lots of spontaneity and creativity will not suit a business trying to develop a solid reputation as a safe pair of hands. It may suit a young children's TV company or a teen fashion designer. Yet designers are often briefed by businesses to come up with something 'creative' that marks them out as being 'different'. Creativity means many different things. To an accountant, it may be finding a way to put one set of figures into a different column. There is a fair chance that the client will hate the results if the designer takes the brief literally.

For example: The brief is for a look that shows you are effective, but down-to-earth and not too garish. One that does not look as if you were throwing money around and suggests you will be good value for money.

The designer would translate this into an understated use of colour, with a straight-forward, clean cut, professional look to underscore your effectiveness. They'd choose a good quality matt paper (not too flash and glossy) with a solid feel, without being over-heavy.

It's no exaggeration to say that paper choice is as important as the design. Cheap looking paper can make good design look nasty. Make sure you see what the design will look like on the suggested paper. Or at least get a blank mock-up made on the paper specified by the designer.

Events

🕐 £/$ ££/$$ 📖 ❝❞ ✶ ⊙

When it comes to client entertainment or running business seminars, there's an almost unlimited range of possibilities. It's not really possible to prepare for all eventualities, but here are a few basic tips:

At all events, the most frequently asked question is: 'Where is the cloakroom?' Make sure all the hosts know where facilities are for both sexes.

Acoustics of rooms change dramatically from empty to full. People soak up sound, so make sure you have a sound system that works well.

All hotel and conference centre equipment is suspect until proven otherwise. Always arrive early to sort out problems.

There's also a law that says the day you forget to arrange coat-hanging facilities is the day the heavens open.

If you are feeding people, check your guests' dietary requirements: allergies and vegetarianism seem to be on the increase.

Exhibitions

🕐 ££/$$ ❝❞ ⊙☺

Try never to exhibit at an event you have not experienced before. Every small business exhibitor I've spoken to regrets the money and time spent exhibiting at something they didn't check out properly. Common complaints include:

- ■ The focus of the whole exhibition wasn't right and no-one, including the organisers, was interested in them
- ■ Competitors were much better prepared and the new small business exhibitor looked unprofessional by comparison
- ■ Their stand was badly sited and few people came to see them

PR TECHNIQUES

At the very least, before exhibiting, go to similar events and check out the standard of other exhibitors. Make sure costs don't contain hidden extras like cleaning, erection charges and basic services like electricity.

You will also need to think up a reason for people to come to your stand. A new product launch should be backed up with leaflets at the entry point, the organiser's press office support and a formal launch at the exhibition. A prize draw from business cards dropped into a box on your stand should also be advertised prominently.

A slot on someone else's stand is a much safer start. Sometimes enterprise support agencies take stands at major craft and trade fairs and invite small businesses to share the space. If you can offer an appropriate theme, the local tourist board or business group may welcome your input to brighten up their stand. Don't swamp your host's efforts in the drive to make a quick sale or word will spread and bring your stand-sharing days to an abrupt end.

Newsletters (see Chapter 11: Going into print)
 🕐 £/$ ££/$$ 📖 🎧 💾 📄 ✉ ☎ ✦ ☉ ☺

Financial Information
✦ ☉

Small companies traditionally play their financial cards close to their chest. There is one group of people that you should always keep informed by routinely sending an end-of-year financial statement: your backers, whether they are family, friends, shareholders, equity stakeholders, venture capitalists, business angels or the bank. Your accountant, lawyer and anyone else advising you would also benefit from being kept up to date.

A short review of the year just ended, together with a forecast of the year ahead, is a good idea. This gets you into practice for the time when you are big enough to seek a listing for your shares on the Alternative Investment Market (UK), EASDAQ (Europe) or NASDAQ (USA). The trick to forward forecasting in businesses of any size is not to give anyone any surprises. If you intend to head for a listing, practise getting guestimates for the year ahead as accurate as possible.

The format for annual reviews and year ahead forecasts is well laid down. A glance at the front section of any large company's annual accounts will give you the basic idea.

For more details, see the investors section in What is PR? on pages 16-17.

Leaflets and flyers
🕐 £/$ ££/$$ 🎧 ☉ ☺

Short leaflets and flyers (single sheet leaflets printed one side only) are sometimes the only way to get a specific message across to a group of people in a short time. If you have a shop with a good throughput of customers, leaflets and flyers can highlight special offers that are not appropriate subjects for most press releases.

Of course, very unusual loss leaders may work as a press release. TVs and three-piece suites for a pound heralding the start of the annual sales used to be regularly featured on national TV news.

To reinforce the image of your business, leaflets and flyers should be designed to fit in with your corporate identity (q.v.).

Lobbying
🕐 📖 🎧 💾 📄 📄 ☎ 66 99 ✱ ☉

It's surprising how effective lobbying can be, particularly at local level. If you want something done in the neighbourhood, or object to a local decision such as a new development, consider mounting a campaign. Lobbying does come with a time warning, however. Once you start, it's hard to stop and you will need to demonstrate commitment and devote a large amount of time to the campaign.

A campaign has three phases: preparatory, launch and conclusion.

1.   Preparatory
Target and plan
In the preparatory stage you will need to identify whom you need to influence.

Canvas extent of support
If it's a matter of objecting to something, sound out the support you have got from all who would be affected. Ask for their input on ways to tackle the problem.

Are enough people affected to launch a campaign?

Is there enough support for a successful petition?

Research
Have the people, or organisations, you are objecting to previously been stopped from doing something similar? What were the most effective arguments used then?

Are there other successful campaigns from which you can learn?

Are there any problems that could stop the development in its tracks, such as overloading water and drainage systems, or the chance of polluting effluent from the proposed new development?

Go to the library to research the council officials involved, the elected councillors, and other relevant officials, along with the names of key people in any company involved.

Contacts

Does anyone have contacts within the local planning office? Or within the company involved?

Celebrities/organisations

Could a famous person or a well-known organisation back the campaign?

Expertise

Do you have any expertise in your camp: free legal advice, expert witnesses of any sort?

Press

Would the local press take up the campaign? Telephone and sound them out.

Put out a pre-launch press release, saying that the campaign is going to be launched on (date).

2.   The launch

If you decide there's enough support, form a committee, think of a campaign title and a logo.

Launch the campaign with press releases to local papers.

Make placards and call a press photocall at the site if that is applicable.

Involve your celebrity or well-known organisation or arrange a visual opportunity for photographers. Make sure your supporters turn up in force with banners and placards. If the people involved are high profile, include radio on your press invitation list.

If you have a strong visual spectacle, send an invitation to local TV stations, including cable and community TV.

Write explaining the position to all those proposing the scheme to which you object and invite them and relevant officials to the launch photocall. Make sure the press know. The press love controversy; the prospect of two sides battling it out with a war of words will bring the reporters along. If the opposition don't turn up, you can adopt the moral high ground. Say you offered them the chance to debate the issue and you are open to discussions.

Distribute petition forms to local shops, businesses and anyone else who meets a lot of people. Keep going round to collect/top up the petition forms and show that the campaign is still active. Discuss it with shop counter staff and anyone else who might be drawn into casual discussion about petition forms sitting on desks or counters.

Keep people up to date. Liaise with your supporters with a brief news sheet and update meetings.

Keep an eye on developments that might lead to a press release or press photocall opportunity.

If appropriate, press for a public meeting with all key players in attendance.

3.   Concluding phase

When you judge the moment to be swinging your way and you have collected an impressive number of signatures, make an event out of presenting the petition to the appropriate person(s). Devise a visual twist – the presence of a celebrity or well-known organisation or a giant photo prop of some sort – to bring press photographers to your photocall.

Research the options: is there a possibility of an appeal if the decision goes against you? What is the next stage?

Await the results of your campaign or pile on the pressure with more visual press photo opportunities or celebrity involvement, depending on the situation, until a decision is reached. Deal with follow-up press interviews once the announcement is made.

What do you do if you win/lose? You can stir up a backlash of public opinion if you and your supporters are seen to be too triumphant, so make sure everyone is magnanimous in victory. If you lose, everyone must know what the next step is, so be purposeful in defeat. Work out short 'soundbites' for the press and TV cameras.

Public meetings

It's rare for a small business to be operating in an area where they will raise issues of public concern. However, if you do end up involved in a public meeting, most of the Presentations section below applies here in terms of speech preparation and anticipating questions.

To keep abreast or current issues, keep an eye on the local press. Make sure that all parties involved get together to plan how to answer objections. Work out in advance who is going to deal with which areas.

Presentations

Most small business owners dread having to stand up and 'sell' their business by making formal presentations. It would be surprising if the business owner was not nervous, for there is so much of the owner invested in a business, and often the deal is so important to the business' future.

The first step is to make your nerves work for you. They will give you an edge and make the adrenaline flow if you really know your material. If you don't, the nerves will show. So prepare, prepare, prepare. Work out what you want to say.

PR TECHNIQUES

Use the 5W questions to plan what you are going to say and anticipate likely questions:

- Who are you? Who's going to be involved?
- What are you going to do for them? What price are you asking?
- When can you do it?
- Where can you operate? (local/national or whatever is relevant)
- Why are you suggesting this solution? (stress the benefits).

Don't forget the How? question:

- How will you set about the task?

Reduce your answers to key messages. From there, reduce these key messages to key word prompts which will trigger the most important points you want to make.

If you can back up each key word with no more than three points or examples – also reduced to key words – you have the framework of a flexible presentation. Suddenly, what looked like four pages of closely-typed paper is reduced to a few words:

KEY POINT
     keyword
     keyword
     keyword

and so on, through half a dozen key points. For example:

KEY POINT: waterproofing
     keyword: seamless
     keyword: standards
     keyword: customers

Reminds you to mention waterproofing as a key issue. Bring up the seamless construction and talk about the seamless design. Mention the fact it complies with rigorous standards which you will name and discuss. NB: Name drop the prestigious customers who have placed massive orders/shown interest

If you are any good at mind-mapping, that is another way of getting a concise overview of the subject in hand, and a highly recommended technique (see Tony Buzan's book, *Use Your Head*, published by BBC Books ISBN 0-563-20811-2 for instructions in mind-mapping).

Use these keywords as your prompts. Practise your presentation to the point where you are comfortable with all its aspects, so you can happily switch back and forth across the whole range of key points. That way, you will not be thrown if you are asked questions that take you off the pre-determined track. A quick glance at your keyword sheet or mind map allows you to take in the whole picture on one page. Practise in front of a mirror or, better still, video yourself.

It is a lot of work the first time you do this, but it's all there the next time you have to make a presentation: all you have to do is adapt it to suit the particular situation.

Pre-pitch

- Choose you team. If others will be involved in handling the business and you think they would make an impressive contribution to the pitch, involve them, too. Find out how many people you will be presenting to and decide whether you need support. It's usually not a good idea to outnumber the people to whom you are pitching.
- If you do involve others, make sure they have a positive role to play in the pitch, and their responsibilities for the job in question are clearly explained. Make sure they know the areas they are to address and the running order you are planning, then all of you should rehearse – several times if necessary. Make sure you don't involve people who will not be working on the business. It will seem odd to the client and you will not be fully trusted when the next contract review comes along.

- Find out how long you have and plan your presentation to allow about half the time for discussion and questions.
- Ask whether you are the first or last. If you have the choice, opt to go first: you will be the measure by whom everyone else is judged.
- Ask how many presentations are being made. If it's a large number and you are on near the end, you will seem like a breath of fresh air if you don't take them step-by-step through their own brief. Virtually all the others will, and it is immensely tedious to sit through the sixth repetition of your own words in one day. If you are on near the end, cut to the chase and show how you'd solve their stated needs.

On the day

- Stick to well-proven speaking aids such as OHPs, slides or computer projections. Have them set up and tested well in advance of the presentation.
- Enter the room with your shoulders back. And smile. Make eye contact with all the people in the room, speak up and stand (or sit) tall. Don't slouch, mumble or fidget.
- Distribute handouts at the end so they are concentrating on you instead of fidgeting with the notes. The handouts should contain bullet points to remind them of your key points and include any background client lists or case histories mentioned in the presentation.
- Remember to have plenty of business cards and always take more copies of everything than you need. We were once told we'd be seeing six people and walked in to face 16. We were glad we had three people on the pitch team and felt sorry for the lone competitors who went in before and after us. Needless to say, we got the job.

Press relations (see Chapters 5, 6,7,8,9 and 10)

Networking

Face to face message delivery is probably the most potent form of selling. Joining a networking body can accelerate the process. Remember that most recommendations come via a third party, so networking is about building up lots of connections with people that support what you are doing and want to do business with you. You will inspire confidence and support if you have a clear vision of what you do and what you want to achieve.

Although it's essential to ensure that everyone with whom you come into contact is clear about what you do, networking isn't about ramming sales messages down people's throats. It's building up a network of supporters. It helps if you approach networking by looking for ways to help other people. You will find this attitude will eventually be reciprocated through third party recommendations.

Apart from the usual Chambers of Commerce and professional bodies, some newer organisations are bringing a refreshing twist to the networking scene. For example:

The CEO Network located in Charlotte, a US professional networking group recently reached a goal to generate $1 million in revenues. The 17-member group meets weekly to hone network skills and to exchange business referrals. Members keep track of the number of referrals they gave and received, and how much business they generated as a direct result. Their scorecards are tallied at the Houston HQ. For information about The CEO Network, call McNeilly at (US) 704 552-8507.

BrainPool, a British business networking group uses innovative learning opportunities to bring people together for positive and productive connections. They have world-wide contacts. Their website is: Brainpool.co.uk. Telephone 0131 229 1576.

Roadshows

🕐 **££/$$ 66 99 ⊙☺**

Roadshows can be anything from travelling exhibition stands mounted in a series of sites, to a series of presentations. They are time-intensive and usually very demanding, involving a lot of travelling, preparation and presentations.

Roadshows are usually undertaken to launch a new product or service, or explain new aspects of a complex situation. Roadshows are particularly good when you need to convey complex material to a number of people in different locations. If you give a short presentation and then take questions, you can quickly clarify misconceptions and pick up a lot of feedback on your products or services. Roadshows allow you to reach a large number of people face-to-face over a tightly-defined period.

A roadshow is a good idea when it's essential that a number of key people in different areas understand an important aspect of a subject. It might be a modification to existing instructions, a new product being introduced to retailers or agents, or a communications exercise to help staff of a client company understand a new system which you are helping to implement or supply. They can be run for customers to introduce a new aspect of a service or product.

The presentations section will help you prepare your material and the section on corporate hospitality will help you set up in different venues and look after your guests.

Double check your travel arrangements: tickets, van hire, hotel/guest house bookings and make sure you have an emergency list of alternative suppliers in case there's a problem.

Carry spares: Sellotape, staple gun, Blu-Tack, scissors, craft knife, notepads, pens and anything else you might conceivably need. Make sure you have got a pager or mobile phone. A thermos flask and emergency rations are a good idea if you are on the move over long distances.

Seminars
🕐 £/$ ££/$$ 📖 🖅 ☎ 66 99 ✶ ☉ ☺

One of the best ways of setting a sprat to catch a mackerel is to run a seminar on a subject on which your business is expert. Lawyers do this with intellectual property issues. At short evening seminars they frighten the life out of attendees with tales of all that can go wrong – and why you need a lawyer. They also take the opportunity to demonstrate their expertise by showing how they saved the day for various clients.

You can team up with others offering non-competing services in the same area by arranging a half-day event and splitting the costs. You will all end up with a good list of people that have expressed interest or attended the event. If you generated press publicity for the seminar, that should have brought in potential clients. It's a good idea to get money up-front for expenses so that you are not left holding the baby if another business pulls out at the last minute. No money, no list...

Open days
🕐 £/$ 66 99 ☉

Who to invite? Whoever you invite, people like watching others work.

- People are nosy: they like to see where partners or parents work and learn more about what they do.
- Customers like to see what makes a business tick and judge for themselves whether they are dealing with a well-run firm.
- Financial backers like to see their money in action.
- If you are anticipating expanding and may need to recruit locally, you might want to invite a class from the local school.

PR TECHNIQUES

So, if you have got suitable premises, or a process that is interesting to watch, or an end product that is good to look at, invite people to see it – unless, of course, there are health or safety reasons not to do so. Make a day of it. If the business isn't interesting to look at, you can celebrate an anniversary or business birthday.

Beforehand

- Check that the details are correct and invitations went out
- Make sure you have got ample cloakroom space
- If appropriate, check car parking arrangements are in hand
- Check that the whole building is in tip top condition
- Put flowers and clean towels in toilets
- Tidy desks
- Clean entrances, approach roads and yards.
- Does the front door need painting?
- Does the signage need smartening up?
- Are there any rooms that could do with a lick of paint?
- Chairs that need recovering, filing cabinets that could do with a re-spray?
- Girlie calendars or obsolete notices to take down?
- Machines to tidy up?
- Displays past their sell-by date?

On the day

- Put up welcoming notices
- Arrange to have people talking about what's going on
- Show groups around
- Show raw products and the finished results
- Talk about the firm's strategy for success, future plans and new markets to conquer
- If you have space for entertainment, from a lone pianist to a magician, put it on
- Could you run a competition, games or a prize draw?
- Don't forget refreshments

Sponsorship

🕐 £/$ ££/$$ 66 99 ✱ ☉

There is a strong tradition of personal enthusiasms overcoming common sense in this field, like the financiers who took clients on one of the UK's most dangerous and difficult off-shore yacht races and ran into terrible weather conditions.

Pretension is another stumbling block. I've seen a major organisation spend large sums of money on a performance given by a world-famous ballet company, but they didn't have a single senior person with a flicker of interest in dance. Neither did the customers they invited. The interval conversation was somewhat stilted.

I have also seen a relatively small sponsorship of a world-famous Italian opera at the Edinburgh Festival be incredibly successful for a local delicatessen. The clamour for publicity and media attention is fiercely intense during what is the world's largest arts festival. However, the contrast of sponsor and sponsored was so delicious that virtually all the broadcast media in town interviewed the sponsors. The deli owners appeared on arts TV shows, radio chat shows and were featured very positively in many newspapers.

Sometimes sponsorships are a way of putting something back into a significant client base. A printer who did a lot of work for educational establishments chose a lesser-known sport to sponsor. They backed the junior national finals for three years, which allowed them to put their name to the title. They picked up more work from contacts made at various stages in the proceedings. They also gained quite a lot of publicity in UK national newspapers, on TV and in the local press. A large part of the sponsorship was 'in kind' (providing goods, not money). They printed the event entry forms, information and match programme, so the actual cash outlay was not heavy.

Getting in at the start of a sport is rewarding if its ethos fits in with your corporate image. In a few years' time, the amounts currently being paid to sponsor national snow-boarding teams will look derisory. Yet snow-boarding, much easier to learn than skiing, has a completely different mass market appeal.

Make sure that other sponsors don't hog the limelight and that you get genuinely useful publicity opportunities to entertain customers or meet key people in return for your support.

Staff Relations

Sometimes PR begins at home. Whether you have one employee or 50, staff are essential to your business and it's a real hassle when good staff leave. Staff stay with companies they feel are successful and involve them in the business.

Motivating the workforce: getting them to the point where they are itching to get into work to try out a new idea is a complex business. Get it right and the bottom line results are almost immediately apparent. Get it wrong and profits plummet.

Of course, staff are motivated by fear of losing their job. But who wouldn't look for something else if put under pressure? Pay and perks are important. To keep staff, and to keep them interested and enthusiastic about their work, means communicating a sense of direction and dynamism – the leader's vision. So include staff in your plans. Talk to them and you will find they have surprisingly good ideas and connections.

Video

⟳ ££/$$ ★⊙☺

Desk-top video editing on PCs has brought the cost down, but video is still an expensive exercise for most small businesses – unless you can persuade someone else to pay. People are used to TV production values: anything less looks cheap and nasty.

In today's pressurised work climate, many corporate videos never see the light of day. Most recipients don't bother to play promotional tapes unless they have a good reason for doing so.

If you are there while they are looking at the video, why aren't you talking to them to find out what they want and how you can provide it? If, however, you are selling something visual that needs a lot of explaining, or involving a process that isn't easy to demonstrate, a well-made short video (under five minutes) may clarify your case.

Short videos on a continuous loop can work at exhibitions in retail outlets and anywhere there's a captive audience, like queues or shop windows at bus stops (as long as it is visually explicit and not reliant on a sound track). But watch that equipment is guarded at all times.

Websites
🕐 £/$ ☉☺

Having a website says you are switched on to new technology and open to world-wide trade. If that fits your image, you will already have a website. If it's not been refreshed for a while, see whether it can be made more attractive to visitors.

- Are there incentives to visit: a competition, a nugget of useful information, or an entertaining experience?
- Are you getting useful information from visitors to your site?
- Is it easy to buy your products or services from the site?
- Have you promoted your site to people who might be interested?
- Are you replying fast enough to visitors' messages and queries?
- Have you registered with all the main search engines?
- Have you negotiated links to related sites?
- Have you checked how it compares with competitors?
- Is your website address on all your stationery and business cards?

PR TECHNIQUES

If you want to get a website up and running, make sure you get it working before you promote it. Check out what it looks like from another computer and make sure it does not take ages to download on an older computer. Get an easy-to-remember web address.

CHAPTER 5

PRESS RELATIONS

But surely newspapers are only interested in big companies?

Speak to any business journalist and they will tell you they are sick of hearing about the same companies. They want to hear about growing companies and innovative new developments.

I know of one relatively small company that has doubled in size every year for 11 years – with no press coverage. Although they were proud that they were doing well, they did not think they were doing anything that was newsworthy. Every business editor we spoke to just about bit our hand off when we told them about a small business with such a dynamic growth pattern. They wanted to run large features on their small business pages to demonstrate how it could be done and encourage others.

It would have cost hundreds of thousands of pounds to buy the editorial space this company was capable of generating though good PR. Even if they had bought the space it would not have been as effective as an editorial mention. Why should this be? Because of the obvious vested interests of advertisers.

Editorial mentions are an independent editorial recommendation or endorsement. They are generally reckoned to have six times the power of an advertisement.

PRESS RELATIONS

Even if you don't have a dramatic meteoric business story to tell, you can still generate thousands of pounds of free publicity in the press. Use the copyright-free press release templates and guidelines in this book. They cover most of the common types of business stories, which you can adapt to suit your business needs.

The great advantage you have over larger companies is novelty. And the media thrive on it. Fresh faces, new ideas, new stories. Present your stories professionally, and they will want to hear about your company. This book shows you how to recognise news opportunities and give your stories the best chance of gaining press coverage.

Editorial and advertising

The contents of any media, whether it is a newspaper, magazine or broadcast, can be categorised as editorial, advertising or advertorial. Naturally, you want to get as much coverage as possible, free of charge, in the editorial section.

There is a lot of confusion between editorial, advertising, and advertorial in the media. Some of this is deliberately caused by over-zealous media advertising sales people, so let us take at look at each category.

Editorial

Editorial is written or commissioned by journalists, broadcasters and editing staff employed by the individual publication or broadcast medium. They regularly conduct research and have a very good idea of what their readers or audience want to read, hear or see. The very survival of paid-for publications depends on giving readers what they want. With so much riding on the quality of stories, editing staff decisions about what goes in are final.

That means you have to interest the right journalists in your story.

Because editorial is independent, it carries that publication or broadcaster's recommendation or endorsement. Research has shown that endorsement effect is worth around six times the effect of advertising.

Editorial is normally independent of advertisers and advertising. The most respected media keep their advertising and editorial departments separate, so that advertisers cannot influence editorial.

Many media advertising salespeople imply they can influence editorial. Keep your wallet firmly locked up unless you like hearing lame excuses after you have parted with your money. If a publication is blatantly led by advertising considerations, few people will bother to read it or be influenced by it. But press cuttings – even from that sort of publication – that mention you and your business are worth collecting for future use.

Editorial is sub-divided into 'news' and 'features'. The best way to trigger a mention in the news section is through an appropriate press release (see next chapter). Address it to the news desk if you have not identified a particular journalist who writes your type of story in your target media.

It's harder to get a feature covering your business but the way to start is with a letter and an outline of the idea you have to interest their readers. Address it to the features editor if it's not aimed at a specific section – sports, business or fashion – for example.

Advertising

Advertising is paid-for space or airtime, the content of which is determined by the advertiser. Once you start sending out press releases, you may well get an increase in calls from media advertising departments. This usually means the publication in question is advertising-led. If you do not want to spend money, just tell them you do not have an advertising allocation in your marketing budget.

Sometimes, there is no alternative to some form of advertising if you are trying to shift old stock quickly or boost sales of something that cannot be remotely described as newsworthy. Remember that most advertising rates are negotiable. Try for at least a third off.

If you do have an advertising budget and you want to make a splash, check out advertising features. This is where a publication will put a page together from your text and pictures, plus supporting advertisements. Some publications will supply a photographer and journalist to help put the feature together.

The resultant page will often be labelled 'advertising feature' or 'special feature' in the top margin.

With an advertising feature, you get much bigger space for the money than with straight advertising: as much as 40% or 50% extra advertising space free. Most papers have a minimum size of a half or full page for an advertising feature, so you will still be spending quite a lot.

Newspapers usually insist that an advertising feature is made up of a selection of supporting advertisements as well as advertorial text. The minimum size they will take is usually half a page; but a full page is more common.

In magazines, you can often dispense with supporting advertisements. The resultant paid-for feature is called an 'advertorial' (see below).

The advertising feature format works well if you are opening new premises and have had a lot of work done by several contractors. If you can persuade them to support the advertising feature by taking space will get a lot of your advertorial space free. Many contractors have seen profits dwindle in this way and no longer support such features. To ensure you have a good adverting feature to launch your new scheme, negotiate the matter with your contractor(s) when you are commissioning the work.

You could team up with a number of non-competing related businesses to run an advertising feature on a topic of mutual interest, with everyone contributing towards the cost. On-the-ball advertising sales people should offer to contact potential advertisers for you.

As long as one advertiser does not hog the advertorial copy at the expense of the others, you have a good start to a fruitful mutual collaboration. Make sure everyone pays up-front if you have to bear the full costs. Advertising departments usually expect payment within two weeks and have no hesitation about taking legal action.

Some examples:

- Home repairers of all kinds could do a *"Home Owners Guide to Renovations"* or *"Preparing for the Big Winter Freeze"*. You could involve any of the related trades: plumbers, joiners, electricians, gas fitters, heating specialists, roofers, chimney specialists, damp proof specialists, cavity wall and other insulation firms, glaziers and double glazing companies, conservatories, landscape gardeners, insurance brokers, banks, other loan providers and local DIY suppliers... No doubt you will think of more.
- Wedding suppliers could get together to do a *"Countdown to the Big Day"* or *"Ten Steps to Wedding Happiness"* or *"20 Ways to Make 'The Day' Perfect"* and involve dress shops, outfit hire specialists, florists, photographers, cake-makers, stationers, shops with wedding list services, car hire, honeymoon hotels and holiday firms....
- Events managers or party planners could bring in their suppliers to run a feature on *"How to Throw the Party to end all Parties"*. It could be adapted to seasonal themes or you could come up with a *"Party Tips Checklist"*. Solicit support from hotels and other venues, caterers,

drinks companies, marquee suppliers, special effects, music, discos, florists, magicians... you name it!
- Design firms, printers, paper brokers and repro houses could team up to do a piece on *"Tips for Better Business Brochures"* or *"Colour Sells"*.

TOP PR TIP: Any business that involves a number of key suppliers can investigate mutual collaborations, from business receptions and sponsorships to advertising features.

Advertorial

Advertorial is a hybrid. It is actually paid-for advertising where you usually supply copy and pictures and the layout design artwork. The point about advertorial: it's designed to look like the main editorial copy. Some media will get their journalists to write the copy for you but practices vary. Before you commit yourself, check out that you are not liable for additional charges like colour separation fees or design costs.

In magazines, a page of advertorial or a double page spread is not uncommon. Broadsheet (larger than tabloid size) newspapers, are more likely to insist on an advertising feature. They have a point. A full page takes thousands of words. Just try and put a full page of text together on the same topic and keep the readers' interest!

With advertorial, you usually have total control, or at least a veto, over the words. The exception is if your advertorial is offensive in some way, in which case the publication can refuse to accept it.

We ran a local Chamber of Commerce magazine where a new member tried to place an advertorial. The text we received claimed they were the only member offering a certain service. We knew another member of the same chamber offered that service; they had advertised the fact in a previous issue. We had to ask the new advertiser to amend the copy for three reasons:

1. The advertisement contravened the UK Advertising Standards Authority rules in that it was clearly untrue.
2. The Chamber did not want to upset the other member.
3. We would not be doing the new member any favours by running that ad. He would have had egg on his face when readers recalled the other company's prior claims.

Local newspapers often have shopping features with a series of advertisers, decked out to look like independent editorial. It's surprising how many people think advertorial is actually editorial; it often works much better than straight advertising.

Nowadays some appointment columns come into the advertorial category because you have to pay for announcements. With other publications, inclusion is at the editor's discretion, and is usually confined to senior executives of fairly large concerns. If you see a lot of salespeople mentioned in an appointments column, and it's not a sales trade magazine, the chances are you pay to get in.

Colour separation charges

A grey area is colour separation charges when publications offer to carry your text free of charge along with a picture of your product. They then mention that the picture costs them money to reproduce, and ask you to help by paying the colour separation charges. Unless you do, your text will not appear.

Now, if the charge just paid for the colour separation, it might be fair enough for a specialist publication to resort to these tactics. We have routinely encountered so-called colour separation charges that are disguised advertising fees. We have been asked for ten times the cost of any colour separations we have paid for at a repro house. You could call their bluff and offer to supply the colour separations just to see the lame 'technical problems' and excuses crawl out of the woodwork.

PRESS RELATIONS

If they accept your offer and you are keen to get a picture into the publication, find out the exact size of the finished reproduced picture. You will need to know what sort of film they need (terms like 'right-reading positive' and 'emulsion side down' should be noted carefully) and the 'number of dots per inch' they require. You will find reprographic services listed in *Yellow Pages*.

Getting into the news pages

There are lots of opportunities to get into the editorial section of the press; news editors and journalists are constantly looking for suitable material to fill their pages. A surprising amount of writers use PR-inspired material sent to a publication in the form of news or press releases. Press releases are announcements sent out by organisations and companies whenever they want to convey news to the media.

You do this by issuing press releases by fax or post or by developing a relationship which enables you to contact journalists on the telephone. You will notice that e-mail is not mentioned. That is because many publications are swamped by them. If a journalist specifically asks you to e-mail, that is entirely different.

How to write press releases is dealt with in the next chapter. This chapter shows you how the journalist works and how you can use that knowledge to get more effective press coverage.

Know your media

The more you understand what the press wants, the easier it will be to place news stories and features. But make sure you spend most of your effort on the publications your customers read. It sounds obvious, but to make sure press coverage gets in front of the audiences you seek, you need to ask your customers which newspapers and magazines they read.

It's worth reading the last three issues of the press you want to get into. Note the editorial and advertising content. In the US, you can get writer's guidelines from the editorial department of the publication concerned. For an additional idea of the type of contributions accepted, look up the publication in the *Writers and Artists Handbook* for the UK media. In *The Writer's Market*, the US equivalent, most editors list what they want from writers.

For regional news, select the regional, local and community press, together with suitable trade or regional magazines.

If it's about opening a local shop or industrial unit, promoting a local person, winning a local order or striking a local deal, it's a story for the local press: newspapers, magazines, radio and possibly TV if there is a strong visual element. Pitch your story at the 'local' and 'community' level rather than going for a wider coverage.

This means drawing up good press lists. There will be more about that later in this chapter.

The competition for news space

Given the huge number of words to fill the average newspaper (about the same number as this book) every day or week, you can see that is a lot of space to fill. All publications are on a news treadmill, having to churn out issue upon issue on a rigid publication schedule.

Even so, the editorial section of newspapers and magazines routinely receive ten times more stories than they can use. To get your story nearer the top of the heap and bring it to journalist's attention is what good press relations is all about.

Over 70 writers can be involved in each issue of a national publication.

PRESS RELATIONS

That means a mixture of work from staff journalists, freelancers, news agencies, contributors, reviewers and letter writers.

First you have to identify which writers on each publication will be interested in your story.

Then you have to respect the enormous time pressure under which journalists work. Accurately handling a book's worth of text at the cutting edge of legal hurdles every day does not do much for their tolerance levels when it comes to time-wasters. Because smaller publications on longer publication schedules are often understaffed, they may be under just as much time pressure.

The trick is to approach press relations in a focused and professional way, with minimum time-wasting. Write the press release clearly, following the guidelines in the press release chapter. Think about what you are going to say and have the three main points boiled down to simple short sentences before you pick up the phone to a journalist.

It's no use expecting every press release to be taken up. That is why you need to get press release writing (discussed in the next chapter) down to a fine art.

News is competitive. The strongest stories on the editor's desk at the deadline win through. The rest are dumped. The day after Diana, Princess of Wales died, there was little space for anything else. That is an extreme example but it illustrates why you may get coverage for a relatively small story one day and a much more important piece of news does not get a look in a few weeks' later.

Look at it over the course of a year. Say you put out ten press releases. Three or four could well lead to coverage in a publication that reaches 15,000 people. That is 15,000 people who have heard about you three or four times in an editorial context. If editorial is generally reckoned to be worth six times the power of advertising, think of what that publicity would cost to buy. That is surely worth time and trouble to get right.

If you send your news releases to a carefully selected but extensive press list, you should do much better than generating coverage in just one publication. With a bit of organisation, you can multiply your news coverage to reach hundreds of thousands of people, so it's worth making up press lists carefully. Carefully pick the press to which you send each release. Match your press lists to suit the subject of your story.

Choose your moment

For maximum effect, release survey data when things are quiet:

Steal a march on the PR agencies and company PR departments. When they are mostly off for the weekend, release your survey data before midday on a Sunday by fax, in time for Monday's papers. And be available for comment on Sunday afternoon.

Other slack news periods when there's less competition for news space include July to September in the UK, when Parliament is in recess, big businesses slow down and many people are on holiday.

The period between Christmas and New Year is another good slot, especially if you come up with a seasonal theme for your survey. One of our clients (an accountancy body) came up with a survey question designed to test the Scrooge qualities of accountants and sent it to the quirkier diary columnists of major UK newspapers. At least it helped dispel the myth that accountants had no sense of humour.

The news window is on a time lock

Many small businesses are lucky enough to get a brief spell of glory in the press, particularly when they start up or win a major order. Once the initial flurry of interest dies down, I am often asked how they can repeat that launch success. The answer is they cannot put the same news out again. Once news is out, it's out; 24 hours later, it's cold porridge. The window of opportunity is wide but it does not stay open for very long.

This case study illustrates the point:

Case study:
The florist's flaw

I was in a florist ordering flowers for a client. When the business owner heard I was in public relations she told me she had won a national flower arranging competition for professional florists. The competition organisers in London had sent the story to her local evening paper, which carried a photo and that was that. Could I suggest how she could get the news into other local papers?

It turned out that all this had happened six weeks previously. Daily newspapers, radio and TV run on a 24 hour news cycle and clear the desks between shifts. A few hours makes a difference to news value, let alone six weeks.

As the professionally-acknowledged best florist in Britain, she could have benefited from huge spin-offs. TV appearances, magazine features, newspaper coverage and extensive trade press articles. I did not tell her that because it was too late.

She obviously did not want to develop a second career.

Even if she did not want a hectic lifestyle, she could have developed display demonstrations and premium-priced training courses.

She would have had extra credibility to raise funds, perhaps to open another branch and maybe eventually franchise the business.

She had not even put a notice in her shop window, or anywhere in the shop, to celebrate her success. This was despite there being three other florists in the area, along with grocers, garages and supermarkets, all selling flowers.

It was not as if the business was missing many tricks. Years later, her shop is still in business, but I have often wondered how much more it could have achieved.

Five ways to get in the press
(When you don't have any news)

1. I feel a survey coming on

One of the most successful ways of generating news is to run a survey: Published findings on a subject relevant to your business is likely to have general appeal.

Almost anything can be surveyed and a good survey stands a good chance of being reported. You may not get much coverage the first time but as your data builds and you repeat the survey, trends or changes give the media scope for comment. Repeat your survey on a quarterly, biannual or annual basis and supply previous data to allow comparisons with the current findings. You can include a column showing the percentage changes. In the case of surveys repeated two or more times a year, you can also include the percentage change over the corresponding period during the previous year.

I have seen surveys of children's pocket money amounts from a building society, local house prices from estate agents and mortgage providers, but there is no reason why you could not survey:

- Lunch prices in your town if you are a restaurant offering a particularly good deal
- Bed and breakfast rates in your area if you run a B&B
- Pub prices or changing drinking habits if you are in the trade
- Seasonable goods, from fir trees at Christmas time (compared with the rest of the year) to school clothes at the start of term, as long as your business has some connection with these items

Surveys are particularly popular with radio news desks. They make them sound short, snappy and authoritative. As your data builds, you may be asked to do a radio interview after releasing a survey.

2. No news? Then comment
Speak out on topical issues of the day that affect your business.
- Health
- Industry
- Education
- Economics
- Transport
- Defence
- Environment
- Foreign trade
- Information Technology
- Weather
- Seasonal subjects

These topics can hit the news big time but you have to keep up with the news and be prepared to act fast.

- Listen to early morning radio news to pick up the big topics.
- Work out a short one or two-sentence response that allows you to relate the topic to your business
- Get on the telephone as soon as possible to journalists and broadcasters you have seen or heard commenting on these issues.
- If at first you do not succeed, make your comments shorter and snappier. Keep trying.

3. Take a letter

Don't forget you can get comments on topical issues into Letters pages. Make sure you comment on current topics related to your business area.

Some small business owners work the letters pages brilliantly. Others fail to do so. Keep your letters down to a couple of short pithy paragraphs, with short sentences and to-the-point comment. Address your letters to the editor and mark them 'For the Letters Page'.

4. Quotable quotes

You can gradually become a source of expert comment in your particular area. Regularly feed in short, quotable quotes to key journalists writing on topical issues relating to your own business area.

Busy journalists on short deadlines often find they cannot get hold of people from larger companies just when they want them. Big companies often do not have personnel available after 5pm but that is when things are hotting up on a daily paper. If you have proved yourself to be on the ball and good at coming up with good, short quotable comments they will start coming to you for contributions. Make sure you have given them your home number. With luck, you will be added to their regular list of people to contact when they are writing about particular subject.

That is when you know you have cracked this PR business!

5. Don't forget radio

Radio needs to break up the presenter's voice with audio variety. Bear in mind that lots of different voices make for radio 'colour'.

That 'audio variety' of sound means there is often scope for short comment or 'sound-bites', ranging from three seconds to in-depth interviews. These opportunities can range from phone-in programmes to pre-arranged interviews with a radio journalist on a topical issue. Interviews can be recorded down the phoneline, in the studio, or down an ISDN line. Sometimes radio interviewers and journalists get comments on issues from people in the street. These short interviews are called 'vox pops'.

Before you pick up the telephone to offer your tuppence-worth, practise getting comments down to really tight, short sentences and phrases.

Ten ways to get onto the features pages

Newspapers and magazines handle large amounts of material by setting aside news pages, which are put together at the last possible minute. Background and 'how to' articles, known as features, are printed on features pages. Because features are generally not time-sensitive they are prepared in advance, usually by a different group of journalists.

TOP TIP: If you are trying to get an article into a publication, address a preliminary outline letter to the 'features editor'. If your article is obviously destined for a specific page – sports, fashion or business, for example – address your letter to the appropriate editor if the publication has one.

Features are in-depth pieces on a specific subject. Many regional and local newspapers and specialist magazines will take submitted expert material, providing

■ It is from a **credible source:** a named member of a company or
organisation engaged in activities relevant to the subject matter.

■ It is free of **copyright restrictions,** that is, you have the copyright as
author and you have not assigned the rights to anyone else. If you
are using a freelance journalist to help you prepare your material,
make sure you have a clear understanding of the copyright
arrangement between you.

■ It is an **'exclusive'** – it has never been published before and you
promise not to offer the same article to anyone else. There is no
copyright on written ideas, only on the way they are expressed. So you
can re-write pieces in different ways for other media, just as long as
they are completely re-written. "10 Tips to Bicycle Maintenance" can
be safely re-written to form the basis of "8 Steps to Bicycle Safety".

Let us go through the features process step by step:

1.   Be a credible source
There is no use offering to write about real estate if you are an aerobics
instructor. But *Ten Ways to Fight Flab, Six Ways to Shed Those Christmas
Pounds* or *Shape Up for Summer* would be perfectly acceptable.

2.   Do it by numbers
Numbered short snappy pieces are popular. You can substitute whatever
numbers you want: Ten Tips to (do something that is related to your
business) or Five Ways ...

An aromatherapist could offer:
■ *Five Ways to Unwind*
■ *Three Revitalising Smells That Really Work*

The real estate agent could try:
■ *Six Sure-fire Ways to Make Your House Sell*
■ *Ten Tips for House Buyers: how to stop your dream home turning out to be a
  nightmare*

- *The Five Pitfalls of Home Buying – and how to avoid them*
- *Five Ways to Increase the Value of your Home*

An occupational psychologist might have some success with:
- *Ten Ways to Beat the Blues*
- *Five Stress-busters that Work*
- *Six Confidence Tips for Job Interviews*

3. Know your market

Study the sort of articles carried by magazines and newspapers to see who would be most likely to want your piece. Look at the articles carried by your local media. If you think you could do something that would fit in, write to the editor or features department.

Even if an editor decides not to use your idea, your letter establishes you as a potential source of future stories in your area of expertise.

When you write offering to do a piece, include a brief outline of the ground you would cover, then follow-up with a phone call.

WEALTH WARNING: Agree the subject matter with the features department before you spend real time or money on the project.

4. The 30-seconds call

With all press contact, be prepared for your letter or other written communication to have been forgotten. Media people get sackfuls of mail so have the key points of your approach fresh in your head to remind them and have another back-up idea handy. You will be lucky if they give you more than 30 seconds on the phone and you need to find out a lot in that time.

If you are on the ball and they are interested, 30 seconds is certainly more than enough:

"I'm the MD of Better Homes Ltd and I wrote offering a 350-word piece on *"Seven Ways To Avoid Winter Damage To Your Home"*. (The other person clearly does not remember.) "The line we took was how to prevent frost damage if you go away at Christmas. It could save your readers a lot of hassle and there would be no charge if our by-line's on the article. We can offer you the article on an exclusive basis. Is that the sort of thing you'd be interested in?" If they say no, ask whether they ever take this type of material. If so, have another feature idea up your sleeve.

5.   Be topical

Keep your ideas topical. If you offer *How to Avoid Winter Damage* in the spring, you deserve all the rejection you will undoubtedly get. But summer drought can create subsidence, so what about: *Is Your House Cracking Up? The Five Signs of Dry Weather Subsidence.* Or you could go for spring or autumn (fall) gale damage: *Five Steps to Prevent Roof Damage This Fall* is one idea.

6.   Hire a professional writer

If writing is anathema to you, hire a freelance journalist who already writes for the publications you want to get into. They will write features and place them for you. It may well cost much less than you think because freelance journalism rates are often low when compared with other professionals. A freelance journalist will certainly cost much less than a PR professional.

The average freelancer's range of publications contacts will be limited to the publications he serves but he will have good contacts within this limited market. Because he is already successfully selling into that publication or radio station, he has a good understanding of what particular editors want.

There is no point in forcing the freelance to include flagrant advertising or trying to dictate how they write the piece.

By writing and placing the article, freelancers can be paid twice: by you and the publication. That is great because it's worth their while to work with you and it's in their interest to help you come up with more material. However, not all publications pay for this type of material.

7. Forget yourself and stick to the subject

Press features often focus on showing the reader how to do something themselves. It's not about you proving how great you are. Instead, take the subtle, but effective approach: show you know the ropes by teaching others. They will come to you when they are out of their depth.

Do not expect to get your business name plastered all over the piece, although the publication should credit you. You may be able to get a mention for your business but you will be lucky if your phone number is included. It is still worth trying.

TOP TIP: You do not get free airtime or newspaper space for thinly disguised advertising. You get free space for sharing your expertise.

A lot of the big accountancy firms and corporate lawyers adopt this approach successfully with business advice contributions.

Unless they have an unusual and sought-after area of expertise, small businesses will not find it easy to get advice pieces into a national newspaper. However, local papers and specialist magazines are often happy to take well-written material that is not advertising puffery. If the local press covers your customer base, it's probably the only publicity you will need.

8. Raise your profile

Offer yourself as a profile candidate to publications that routinely run business profiles. The top regional newspaper in our area has an 18-month waiting list of interviewees. You can leapfrog the queue if you have got something topical to say.

"Environment Company MD Sounds Warning on Euro Rules" could work as a short news piece on impending legislation. Or it could be developed into the start of a profile if you have a long history in this area. Why not do both?

As with features, a short letter and outline of the ground to be covered is the best way to start.

9. State your case
Case studies are in-depth articles on a business achievement.

It could be breaking into a foreign market: I know a jewellery designer who did just that through a chance contact made on holiday. It's unusual for a one-woman business to be an exporter so her experiences made a good inspirational feature. The items she made were photogenic, which helped gain her more space. She has also sold pieces to well-known people, which was an excuse for even more photographs. It all formed the basis of a nice colour supplement feature in a regional Sunday newspaper.

Again, a letter is the best way to start.

10. Be exclusive
Because there is keen competition between publications and media groups, exclusive material has more value than an article that is been touted around half a dozen media. Find different angles on your main themes and if you agree to supply a piece on an exclusive basis make sure you keep your promise not to give it to anyone else.

Generating sustained press interest

Small businesses often find they get a blast of free publicity when they start-up, then nothing. So how do you keep generating sustained press coverage?

- Keep finding fresh angles on your business, its products or services
- Maximise press interest in newsworthy events (see the next chapter)
- Comment regularly on topical issues through letters, phone calls and short (one or two) sentence faxes
- Develop good ideas for features

Giving your press cuttings 'legs'

Copies of favourable trade press cuttings will give customers and potential customers confidence in your business. So, show them! Caption the cutting with the publication name or a copy of the publication's masthead. Mount the cuttings on to display boards or frame them. Put them up on the wall. Put photocopies in with your sales letters and presentation materials. I have seen sales reps using clean copies of press cuttings that were several years old.

Of course, once you start getting coverage in the main media, you will give it the star treatment, too.

CHAPTER 6:

COMPILING PRESS LISTS

If you have won a ground-breaking order with a major corporation and it's a UK or American first, you have a local, regional press and national media opportunity.

Press List Checklist

For that sort of story, be prepared to draw up a press list including:

- National daily and Sunday newspapers
- National TV
- National radio
- National press agencies
- Main national business magazines
- Your regional daily and Sunday newspapers
- Your regional and local business magazines
- Your regional TV stations (terrestrial and cable)
- Your regional radio stations
- Your local weekly newspapers
- Local TV
- Local radio
- Your specific trade, technical, business or professional magazines (local, regional and national)
- Other related trade press

COMPILING PRESS LISTS

■   Relevant consumer magazines (local, regional and national)
■   Community newsletters or newspapers

NOTES:
National = countrywide
Regional = main geographic area eg the North West of England; the West Coast of the USA or state
Local = your town or general area
Community = immediate area, usually within a town

Press list sources

You will find local and regional press listed under appropriate headings in *Yellow Pages*.

Scan copies of the press and see who is listed as the editor.

Some of the larger local press follow the national press example of having regular editors and writers for different sections. If you have a sports story, find out the sports editor's name. If all else fails, ring and find out where to send sports stories. Same goes for fashion, health, business, etc, if the publication has a regular page devoted to these and other topics. If it's a small local weekly paper, chances are it's put together by 'the editor and his dog'. So send it to 'the editor'.

Make a point of collecting useful press names and compiling an easy-to-use press list with telephone numbers and mailing or fax labels. We routinely send 80 to 100 releases when we are dealing with an average regional news story. A local release can go to 40 writers.

That is because we send it to all the writers we know who may be interested; that might include five writers who contribute to the same newspaper. Why? Because if one of them is away, you cannot rely on journalists to cover for each other or pass stories around. They are too busy. If you want to reach anyone on a specific area in the press, address your release to 'the business desk' or 'the fashion editor.' If you are not sure, send it to 'the editor' but do not hold your breath.

The national press is often easier to work with because they tend to say who is in charge of each section.

With radio and TV, get the names of the people that present the programmes. If you listen and watch carefully, you will pick up the name of the producer or researcher, to whom the release should be addressed.

The trade press

When people talk about 'the press' or 'the media', the tendency is to think about the newspapers and magazines you see on the news stands, plus TV and radio. Small businesses often neglect or undervalue their most likely press coverage source: the trade press.

There are thousands of trade and technical journals covering just about every known aspect of trade, commerce and industry. (See below for a subject list and the numbers of publications in the UK). These publications are so subject specific that they are often hungry for appropriate stories.

While publications vary enormously in terms of quality, mentions in trade press are often much more valuable than they appear at first sight.

The trade press is assumed to have extra credibility because editorial staff are specialists in their field. That is why:

■ Trade press coverage will enhance your business or professional status in whatever area you operate

COMPILING PRESS LISTS

- **Trade press coverage will give customers and potential customers confidence in your business**
- **Trade press cuttings are respected by mainstream journalists**

So, even if the trade newspapers and magazines in your particular field look a bit rough and ready, it's worth taking time and trouble to get into them. You can always caption and mount your press cuttings, then photocopy them and distribute them as far they will go. Used well, press cuttings will go on working for you for months and years.

Use press cuttings in:

- Sales presentation folders
- Sales letters
- Sales literature
- Exhibition panels or on walls

It's well worth distributing your releases to the most extensive trade press list you can compile. There is always more trade press than you think. To see the full extent of the opportunities, get hold of a media directory and take time to research all the relevant publications in your field.

All PR specialists have their favourite media directories and hotly dispute the relative merits and demerits of each. Contact details for media directories is in the Appendix. We have used *PIMS, Editors, TwoTen* and *PR Planner.* We like *PIMS* for financial PR; we prefer *PR Planner* for trade press and UK regional media. They also do a European and North American edition.

PR Planner code trade and technical journal listings, showing at a glance the type of material editors normally consider for publication. Their Editor Coding gives a good insight into the type of material journals are looking for. While 'financial news' only applies to larger companies, all other categories can be exploited just as easily by inventive small companies who really want press coverage.

PR Planner editor coding

1. NEW PRODUCTS – Equipment, materials and processes. Most journals listed in the directory carry publicity under this heading. Many magazines key new product announcements to a reader enquiry service, which is often a pre-paid card making it easy for readers to apply to the journal for information.

2. PERSONNEL NEWS – Staff changes, obituaries, etc. Many trade journals devote a page to appointments, and editors particularly welcome short announcements of two or three lines. Institute journals generally are interested only in appointments as they affect their members.

3. FINANCIAL – Company affairs. Reports of annual meetings, chairmen's statements, profit forecasts and other financial news are of interest to many publications. Dividend announcements, new issues, etc, are generally required only where financial news is a featured item.

4. TRADE LITERATURE – Reviews of manuals, catalogues, bulletins, etc. Many opportunities exist for publicity for all types of trade literature. Some journals give a full description of new booklets, handbooks, etc, for which they need original copies of the material. As with new product announcements, many journals offer a reader enquiry service covering items in this section.

5. PHOTOGRAPHS – Not all journals use photographs but this directory shows at a glance those which do.

5a. COLOUR TRANSPARENCIES – Apart from indicating the use of photographs, many journals now print photographs in colour.

5b. COLOUR SEPARATION Some journals make a charge for colour separation. This code shows those publications which have indicated to us that they do NOT make a charge.

COMPILING PRESS LISTS

6. LETTERS TO THE EDITOR – Provided they have a definite interest to readers, most magazines will publish letters to the editor.

7. BOOK REVIEWS -This heading refers to books that are on general sale to the public.

8. COMING EVENTS – Meetings, conventions, exhibitions. Some magazines run a regular diary column, often consisting of a listing without editorial description. In such cases editors welcome additional material as background information.

9. CONTRACTS – Projects, contracts awarded, etc. Where editors specify an interest in contracts, considerable scope exists for material relating to announcements of new projects, particularly in the construction field, and contracts awarded. News of tenders invited is sometimes included but most journals carry such information in the form of classified advertising. Abbreviated announcements are often suitable.

10. INDUSTRIAL FILMS – Reviews or news, of industrial, business or educational films come under this heading. Many journals list new films available in the form of an announcement without including any editorial description.

11. ENTERTAINMENT – Theatres, clubs, etc. Openings for publicity in this category exist in a number of journals, particularly if it is tied in with conferences, etc, where delegates may want to know "where to go".

12. GENERAL NEWS – Material about companies, organisations, plant extensions, dealer appointments, etc, give opportunities for a wide range of general releases. Journals with a regional interest particularly welcome local news under this heading.

13. BY-LINED ARTICLES – eg contributions by a member of a company. In most cases 'signed' articles are accepted only on an exclusive basis. Editors of technical journals frequently welcome articles by qualified

contributors. In certain classes of journal, case histories are especially suitable and can provide a valuable publicity outlet.

14. CASE STUDY MATERIAL – Where case study material is indicated, a short application story about equipment, or plant and control in action, is acceptable by prior arrangement with the editor.

Editors' Codes reproduced courtesy of PR Planner

Trade press: scope of opportunities

At the time of publication, *PR Planner* listed 64 general classifications of trade press, with the following numbers of publications in each category:

Subject	Publications
Agriculture and Farming	146
Air Treatment and Heating	25
Antiques	10
Applied Science and Laboratories	62
Architecture and Building	150
Aviation and Aeronautics	84
Baking and Confectionery	9
Catering	45
Ceramics, Pottery and Glass	17
Chemicals	39
Church and School Equipment	8
Clothing and Textiles	50
Co-ops	3
Commerce, Industry and Management	330
Communications, Advertising and Marketing	175
Computers and Automation	278
Construction, Public Works and Civil Engineering	87
Decorating and Paint	12
Defence	35

COMPILING PRESS LISTS

Subject	Publications
Electrical Appliances, Radio and TV	20
Electrical Industry	40
Electronics	163
Energy	52
Engineering and Machinery	113
Fancy Goods, Gift Trade	13
Finance and Economics	375
Food Trade	75
Footwear	10
Furnishings	17
Garden Supplies and Produce	21
Gas Industry	10
Hairdressing	8
Hardware	7
Import and Export	14
Laundry and Dry Cleaning	2
Legal	125
Licensed Trade	40
Marine and Shipping	98
Materials Handling	24
Medical and Health	308
Metal Industry	42
Mining and Quarrying	28
Miscellaneous	92
Motor Trade	60
Municipal and Local Government	144
Music Trade	35
Office Equipment	14
Oil and Petroleum	57
Packaging and Bottling	31
Paper	14
Pharmaceuticals and Chemists	41
Photographic Trade	18
Plastics and Rubber	22

Subject	Publications
Printing and Stationery	27
Publishing	57
Regional Business and Chambers of Commerce	186
Retailing and Wholesaling	40
Safety	83
Timber, Wood and Forestry	22
Tobacco	2
Toy Trade, Sports Goods and Equipment	23
Transportation	98
Travel and Tourism	38

Press release distribution

Faxing: A warning. Sometimes newsrooms get so hectic that a reporter will grab a fax, and a load of others besides. About a third of all faxed material routinely goes astray in newsrooms. Be prepared to re-fax material if a publication says they have not received it.

You might think that post is better. For monthly or weekly publications, it probably is, unless you are on their deadline.

However, media on a 24-hour news cycle (daily papers, TV and radio) is different. **Fax or telephone** news stories to daily media. If you post it, they will assume it's out of date before it got to them. Radio in particular really is an incredibly immediate medium.

I have telephoned a news item to a regional radio station and heard it come over the air before I finished the phone call.

E-mail is sometimes effective and it's easy to reach lots of publications once you build up your list. Some journalists are completely swamped by e-mail messages and don't bother to read them. Basically, individual work practices come into play. If in doubt, ask.

Wire services tend to send masses of major news. A press release from a small business is likely to get swamped among world news headlines and general business news traffic.

The mix: No one distribution method is ideal and we'd recommend building up lists allowing you to distribute through a variety of channels according to the type of media and preferences of individual journalists.

Media directories

You will find press lists in specialised press directories expensive to buy, but they are usually available in public libraries. Press directories include *PR Planner, Editors, TwoTen* and *PIMS* media guides in the UK. *PR Planner* also does a European and a North American version. A copy of *BRAD* (British Rates and Advertising Data) is better than nothing, but because it focuses on advertising data, addresses and telephone numbers may not take you into the editorial team beyond, in some cases, the name of the editor.

If you are feeling flush, many media directories come in CD-ROM, but to obtain them in a form that can be fully manipulated is very expensive. (Some will not allow mailmerging, for instance).

Wire services

PR Web – at http://www.prweb.com/. PR Web is maintained by TOPsites.net, Inc. of Hamilton, Texas and Adrian&Peterson Incorporated of Westland, Michigan.

PR Web's free services allow visitors to post press releases, conduct key-word searches of its press release database, post by-lined articles that are linked to the authors' web sites, participate in threaded discussions with other communication professionals, list new web sites in top Internet search engines and indexes and visit the newest websites which are now on the Internet.

PR Web's value-added paid services simplify the process of creating and distributing press releases. Its Automated Online Press Release Factory will guide novices through the creation of 15 common press releases. These releases can be distributed locally, regionally, nationally or globally directly via the PR Newswire. Based in New York, PR Newswire (http://www.prnewswire.com) is the leading source of full-text news from corporations worldwide for media, business, the financial community and the individual investor.

When not to seek press coverage

Raising your business profile in the press tends to magnify the bad points along with the good. So think carefully before leaping into press relations. The chapter on PR Planning shows you how to assess your situation.

The chapter on PR techniques comes up with many other effective PR alternatives to press relations.

CHAPTER 7:

WRITING PRESS RELEASES

GOLDEN RULES OF WRITING SUCCESSFUL PRESS RELEASES

Golden Rule 1: Success words – the golden news test

What is news? News is the plural of new: if it's new, it's news.

News implies change: something happens – a business is started up, a product is launched, an appointment is made, a deal is struck, a contract is won.

Any news is a potential press release, but how do you find out whether you have news?

Try the success words test
These are words we have collected from press releases that made the news. I'm sure you will find others to add to the list. Make sure they imply success, change and action, or you will slip into the superlatives.

If you cannot apply at least one of these words to the piece of news you want to distribute, you probably do not have a story that will appeal to the media.

WRITING PRESS RELEASES

- addition
- anniversary
- will announce/announces/announced/announcement
- appointment
- award
- best-selling
- breakthrough
- celebrate/celebrations
- ceremony
- change
- complete/completion
- deal
- development
- enhance/enhances/enhanced
- event
- expand/expansion
- extend/extension
- fierce competition
- first in (name appropriate business or industrial sector)
- first in (name appropriate geographic area):
    - local area
    - region
    - county or state
    - country
    - geographic area like Australasia, the American continent, Australasia hemisphere (northern or southern)
    - the world
- increase/increases/increased
- launch/launches/launched
- milestone
- new (possibly in combination with other success words like 'new breakthrough'
- new (product)
- new (service)

- number one
- will open/opens/opened/is opening
- order (as in winning a trade order)
- record breaking
- revolutionary
- stunt
- success/successful
- survey results
- unveiled
- win/won/winning
- world first

Use at least one of these words to inject dynamism into the opening sentence of your press releases.

This opening sentence example contains four news words:

"Manchester-based XYZ company today **announces** a **new** waterproof **addition** to their range of **best-selling** stationery products.

or, even better, six news words:

"**Award-winning** Manchester-based XYZ company **unveiled** a **breakthrough** in stationery products today with the **launch** of their **revolutionary** waterproof range of pre-printed forms: a **first** in the UK.

Golden Rule 2: The essential five Ws

The above examples of news words are contained in sentences that obey the other crucial rule of news writing: the five Ws.

Who?
What?

Where?
When?
Why?

WHERE? Manchester-based
WHO? XYZ company
WHEN? **today** announces a
WHAT? new waterproof addition to their range of best-selling stationery products. (The rest of the release will go on to say WHY?)

Another useful question will help you develop the story:

HOW?

Case study:
A press releases for services

Business owners who are service providers often say at the start of our DIYPR courses that they can see how easy it would be to make a product newsworthy. It's much harder to promote an intangible service.

We say, what about accountants?

With apologies to accountants who are exciting at heart, DIYPR course delegates usually agree that accountants are even harder to promote than their own business. That is because accountants have a dull image; they are perceived as offering the same sort of services. We say, if we can make an accountant newsworthy, we can turn anything into a press release.

So, for service business owners everywhere and accountants in particular, here goes:

"Birmingham accountant John Smith & Co. today **announces** a **new** Tax Savers service for small businesses."

The release could go on to describe the small business accountancy package: it could include a free Tax Saver one hour initial consultation (which gives the accountant a great new sales platform).

For new small business Tax Saver customers, the service could include an appropriate free offer. Perhaps the choice of a book or software that is particularly good at helping small business owners get to grips with their finances? Or a small business magazine subscription? (Do a deal with publishers or software providers to keep costs down.) Costs can be added on to fees. Spread over a year, the extra cost will be virtually undetectable.

For a bit of extra effort, an ordinary service is turned into potential free publicity. The accountant is established as a specialist in a small business niche.

TOP TIP: The trick is to treat a service like a product – by giving it a brand name and throwing in a few appropriate offers to make it specifically suitable for the target market.

If that accountant had a lot of restaurant customers and wanted to target more of that specific market, he might aim his press release at a trade magazine for restaurateurs. He could start the release:

"Good news for Birmingham restaurants"

Birmingham accountant John Smith & Co. today **launched** a **new addition** to their popular range of Tax Saver services: the Restaurant Tax Saver, with a free tax consultation for restaurateurs."

The release would go on to say that John Smith & Co. have a number of core restaurant clients. Helped by their experience in this sector, they have spent months developing a specialised tax service for restaurateurs.

The Restaurant Tax Saver might include a free offer for customers using the service, such as a book on portion control or a subscription to a restaurant trade magazine (contact customers to see what they would recommend or value for a free offer).

The release could not only be sent to the local press and business magazines. It could become a mailshot: a 'restaurant news flash' to all restaurants in the area. The news flash could be dropped into restaurants whenever convenient.

The same technique would apply if the accountant wanted to narrow the market down even more, although the free offers would need to be quite inventive: to fish n' chip shops, to Chinese, Indian or Asian restaurants, to baked potato shops, to Italian pasta houses, etc.

The field is now so narrow that the news release may work better as a flyer than as a press release. But, believe it or not, there are several trade magazines aimed at fish and chip shop owners. Local newspapers and business magazines might pick up the story on a slow news day.

If they wanted to go after larger businesses, the accountant could always put out an announcement:

"Birmingham accountant, John Smith & Co. today **launched a new addition** to their popular range of Tax Saver services: the Midi Tax Saver aimed at medium-sized businesses (companies with an annual turnover of more than £250,000)."

The same sort of sector-specific techniques could be employed as demonstrated above for the small business sector, as long as the book or magazine offers are suitably appropriate.

Golden Rule 3: Strip out superlatives

Once you have written your text, strip out the superlatives: adjectives like 'wonderful' and 'brilliant' are your (biased) opinions and will irritate fact-driven journalists. Superlatives don't belong in the world of news. Because they are so over-worked, it's unlikely that people pay much attention to them anyway.

If you want free space on news pages, you have to play by the news rules. If you want superlatives, buy advertising space.

Golden Rule 4: Personalise the release to the target media

A local newspaper serving a local community rarely carries news that cannot be related to their readership area. That is how a famous apocryphal headline came about:

ABERDEEN MAN DROWNS
Titanic Sinks

Local media know their audience. Local radio stations, for example, find that their listeners get irritated if they carry news of offers or events outside their local area. So they don't.

TOP TIP: Turn the media's hunger for local connections to your advantage. If you want local press coverage, give them a local connection right up front in the headline and first sentence.

Keep the publication's readership in mind and make sure you relate your headline to it. Do not bury impeccable local connections at the bottom of the release or expect the press to make the connection from your address. Do not leave anything to chance.

An average press release gets a three-second scan from a busy journalist, who rarely reads past the first sentence.

In the same way, the trade press are looking for something in their specialised field. Don't wait until the third sentence to bring out the fact that it's a specialised widget aimed at the whatsit market. If you want coverage in the biological scientific press, get the fact that it's a **biological** breakthrough into the headline.

Golden Rule 5: Lay it out professionally

Ten steps to professional press releases

There's a set format that makes it easier for journalists to handle your story, giving them space to mark it up for editing. When there's a rush on (and there nearly always is), they will pick out well-presented releases and ditch long-winded close-packed screeds of text.

1. Send press releases on your **printed letterhead** with the addition of a very large **PRESS RELEASE** notice at the top. In case you need to photocopy this notice onto your letterhead, we have included large 'press release' lettering to copy at the end of the book.

2. Put the **date** of the release at the top, clearly visible. Undated releases will be assumed to be out-of-date as far as news content is concerned.

3. Keep your release down to a **single page,** including contact details at the foot. That means an upper limit of 150 to 200 words. You can add background notes on a separate sheet.

4. The standard advice used to be: use **double spacing** for the text to leave room for hand-written edits. With modern scanning equipment, text is often amended on screen and multiple pages are a pain to scan. Compromise and stick to one page of well-spaced text.

5. **Keep sentences short** and to the point.

6. Leave a two-inch (4cm) left-hand **margin** for editing notes.

7. Use the word **'ENDS'** when the release finishes – see template on page 133 for positioning.

8. Always include at the foot of the main press release, details of who the press should contact for **further information:**
   For further details contact:
   (your name) plus (your phone number – day and evening)
   Include this information, even if it repeats the telephone number on your letterhead: journalists don't waste time searching out telephone numbers.

If you have a mobile phone number and/or a pager number, include that, too.

Add your e-mail number if you have one.

9. For **TV or radio** stations you can add a further 'note to producers' offering to be interviewed eg

   Note to Radio Producers

   From 10am to noon tomorrow (adding the date), Joe Bloggs, MD of XYZ Co. is available for interview or comment

10. Make sure whoever's name is quoted at the foot of the release for further information is available to answer calls for 24 hours after the press receive it. It's amazing how many people issue a release, complete with contact details, but are not available to answer questions when a journalist calls. That is one of the quickest ways to get yourself into a journalist's bad books.

Golden Rule 6: Keep building your reputation

Remember that positive press coverage will keep building and magnifying your image. Keep including key business messages in your press releases. If you can truly claim to be anything like the following, make sure it's mentioned in every release.

- Britain/America's leading XYZ supplier
- The leading XYZ supplier in the region/state
- The leading XYZ supplier in the Chester area

Even if you are not an industry leader, surely you have a reason to justify being:

- A leading supplier in the (country, region, area, county or town)?

Even if your claim does not always get published, you are building your reputation with journalists. But remember, journalists are sharp cookies. The fastest route to a journalist's round file on the floor is claiming something that is clearly untrue. Apart from serious damage to your reputation, you will never be trusted by that journalist again.

CHAPTER 8:

TEN PRESS RELEASE TEMPLATES

This section contains ten sets of notes, templates and examples for small business press release opportunities.

The examples included are based on real events that successfully gained press coverage. However, the facts have been changed to create fictional press releases.

No example is more than 200 words, including contact information at the foot.

1. New products and services

Notes

New products or services are probably your most important news material. They are excellent reasons to issue a press release.

Think about developing a range of products or services, with variants of existing products and services aimed at different types of customer: 'niche markets'. Give each variant a separate but related brand name, as in the accountancy Tax Saver Range example on page 121.

Launch each service, with a decent time interval between, to give you extra chances for press coverage.

TEN PRESS RELEASE TEMPLATES

The release should follow the Six Golden Rules on pages 117 to 127:

1. Use success words
2. Wrap up as many answers as you can to the 5W Questions in the first sentence. (WHO? WHERE? WHAT? WHEN? WHY? – see case study examples on page 120)
3. Strip out the superlatives
4. Personalise the release for the media
5. Follow the ten-step guide to professional press release layout on pages 125-6
6. Build your reputation with key messages

The answers to the WHY? question is often best addressed in the second and third sentences.

Use a new paragraph for the WHY? part of the release. News columns, being narrow, look better with text broken up into one or two short sentence paragraphs.

When developing the rest of your release with your answers to the WHY? question, concentrate on the novel aspects of your product or service.

- Why is it different?
- Why is it better?
- Why is it new?
- Why is it innovative?
- What gives it that extra spark?
- Why did you launch it?

If there is nothing new about it, you do not really have a reason to put out a press release.

On the other hand, you may have a national press release on your hands.

Is it unique?

Can you claim:

- A world first?
- First in Europe? (or any other major area?)
- A UK first? (or any other country?)
- A first on the West Coast? (or any other major area?)
- First in the north east? (or any other region?)

'Firsts' can be quite basic. A new type of soap or cosmetic: a new service for lawyers or laundries; or indeed any other trade or profession, industrial or commercial sector you have targeted.

If you get into firsts, the *Guinness Book of Records* could give you great ideas for extra publicity. You could go for a world record in something related to your business.

Bring in a quote if it contains further useful information.

The last sentence of the release should wrap up the 'How do I get it' details: whom to contact for sales.

Keep releases down to a few short sentences (four or five is ideal). Any further information can be on a separate sheet called 'technical specifications' or 'background notes', depending on the subject matter.

TEN PRESS RELEASE TEMPLATES

Template 1. New product or service launch

(Fill in the brackets and print on your letterhead under a large 'PRESS RELEASE' heading)

(DATE)

(HEADLINE)

(TOWN/AREA) – based (YOUR BUSINESS NAME) today launched a new (PRODUCT OR SERVICE) aimed at the (TYPE OF CUSTOMERS) market.

The new (NAME OF PRODUCT OR SERVICE) is (LIST UNIQUE CHARACTERISTICS)

(QUOTE)

(KEY REPUTATION MESSAGE)

('HOW DO I GET IT?' DETAILS)

ENDS

For further details contact:
(YOUR NAME) at (DAY AND EVENING TELEPHONE DETAILS, PLUS MOBILE OR PAGER NUMBERS AND E-MAIL)

(EXAMPLE 1: NEW PRODUCT LAUNCH PRESS RELEASE: 198 words)

XYZ Company

XYZ House, Any street, Any town, any Post or Zip Code.
Any telephone and fax numbers and e-mail

PRESS RELEASE

20 January 1999

Birmingham bakery announces slimming breakthrough
Having your cake and losing weight*

Birmingham-based XYZ Company today launched a ground-breaking range of cakes aimed at slimmers throughout the UK.

Slimfast cakes are the first in the UK with 90 per cent less fat than their average counterparts.

Joe Bloggs, XYZ's managing director, said: "We're patenting a new bakery process which allows us to cut the fat to well below any other cake on the UK, market".

XYZ, founded five years ago, has rapidly expanded to become one of the Midland's leading wholesale suppliers of ready-made bakery products.

Slimfast cakes come in three varieties: ginger and orange; madeira; and fruit. They are retailed at a suggested 99p per packet in selected health food shops throughout the UK.

Slimfast cakes are also on trial in supermarkets throughout the West Midlands.

The aim is to distribute throughout UK multiples before the end of the year.

For further details contact Jean Smith, sales manager on 0123 456789.

* if used as part of a calorie-controlled diet.

ENDS

For further details contact:

Joe Bloggs, managing director, XYZ's Company, direct on 0123 445678 (day) or 9876 54321 (evening). Mobile: 0321 321321.

2. New business wins

Notes

If you win a major piece of new business, send out a release. If you are appointed a dealer or given a licence for a well-known product or service, let the press know.

People like to deal with people who are successful. American businesses are good at shouting about their successes but small British businesses have a tendency to hide their light under a bushel.

If you mention a client company by name, make sure you have their agreement to do so. A new business relationship could fall at the first fence if you take their name in vain.

If the client or customer is willing to give you an endorsement, include it as a quote: third party recommendation is far better than blowing your own trumpet.

Remember to follow the Six Golden Rules on pages 117-127:

1. Use success words
2. Wrap up as many 5W Questions as you can in the first sentence (WHO? WHERE? WHAT? WHEN? WHY? – see case study examples on page 120)
3. Strip out the superlatives
4. Personalise the release for the media
5. Follow the ten-step guide to professional press release layout on pages 125-6
6. Build your reputation with key messages

Answers to the WHY? questions are often best addressed in the second and third sentences.

With new business wins, it's particularly powerful if you can answer the WHY? question with a quote from the customer: WHY they bought your product or service or WHY have they appointed you as a dealer, licensee or franchisee.

When developing the rest of your release with answers to the WHY? question, bring out aspects of your product or service that make it different from others.

- Why is it different?
- Why is it better?
- Why is it new?
- Why is it innovative?
- What gives it that extra spark?

The last sentence of the release should wrap up the 'How do I get it?' details: price, where it can be bought or whom to contact for sales.

Keep releases down to a few short sentences (four or five is ideal). Further information can be included at the foot under 'technical specifications' or 'background notes'.

Include the client's contact details if appropriate (see example).

Template 2. New business wins

(Fill in the brackets and print on your letterhead under a large 'PRESS RELEASE' heading)

(DATE)

(HEADLINE)

(TOWN/AREA) – based (YOUR BUSINESS NAME) today announced they had signed a new deal to supply (YOUR CUSTOMER'S NAME) with (NAME OF PRODUCT OR SERVICE PLUS AMOUNT CONTRACT IS WORTH IF SIGNIFICANT)

(YOUR CUSTOMER'S PERSON AND JOB TITLE) said "(QUOTE)"

(LIST UNIQUE DETAILS OF PRODUCT OR SERVICES)

('HOW DO I GET IT?' DETAILS)

ENDS

For further details contact:
(YOUR NAME) at (YOUR DAY AND EVENING TELEPHONE DETAILS, PLUS MOBILE OR PAGER NUMBERS AND E-MAIL)

(CLIENT PRESS CONTACT AND CONTACT DETAILS)

(EXAMPLE 2: NEW BUSINESS WINS PRESS RELEASE: 196 words)

XYZ Company

XYZ House, Any street, Any town, Any Post or Zip Code.
Any telephone, fax numbers and e-mail

PRESS RELEASE

20 January 1999

Newcastle firm signs deal with well-known company

Newcastle-based XYZ Company today announced the signing of a £250,000 deal with Wellknown Car Co. to supply XYZ's customer care software, NiceDay, to every branch of Wellknown in Europe.

NiceDay is XYZ's unique computer program that analyses the non-verbal signals we all give out. Working in conjunction with video cameras, it analyses body language and facial expressions, measuring individual salespeople's performance against top sales performers. The software produces a printout showing areas to developed.

The deal is a breakthrough into the automobile sector for XYZ, leading suppliers of sales-related software to the banking and financial sector.

Jim Smith, Wellknown's sales director said: "We chose *NiceDay* because we believe it will significantly improve our salespeople's relationship with customers. Quite simply, there's no other product like it."

For more information about *NiceDay,* contact Julie Brown at XYZ, on 0123 445566.

ENDS

For further details contact:
Joe Bloggs, managing director, XYZ's direct on 0123 445678 (day) or 9876 54321 (evening). Mobile: 0321 321321 or
Jim Smith, Wellknown's sales director on 0234 555555 (day)

(Technical notes enclosed)

3. Winning an award

Notes

An award of almost any kind is an external endorsement of your company and its staff – and worthy of a press release.

Quite often the awarding organisation's own PR professionals will issue a release of their own. It's tempting to think "Oh well, they're the experts, I'm in safe hands". But the professionals will quite rightly serve the person that pays them. They will write the release from the awarding body's perspective, possibly giving your company's name a once-only mention, with no details about what you do.

They will distribute the release where their clients want it to go. A casual assurance that it's going to the regional media in your area may mean they are sending it to a couple of newspapers. From a London or New York perspective, that may mean dealing with the local press. You should build up a much more detailed press list if you follow the advice in this book.

The 'florist's flaw' case study on page 94 is a cautionary tale of what can happen when you are involved in a national competition. Do not make that mistake.

At the very least, make sure you see a copy of the release before it goes out and ensure that it contains a sentence or two or a direct quote from you about your company. Make sure they distribute to your press list or ask if you can issue your own regional release. Check out their trade press distribution, too.

Try and ensure the release includes a judge's quote on WHY they selected your business as the winner.

If you are putting out the local release yourself, remember to follow the Six Golden Rules on pages 117-127:

1. Use success words
2. Wrap up as many 5W Questions as you can in the first sentence (WHO? WHERE? WHAT? WHEN? WHY? – see case study examples on page 120)
3. Strip out the superlatives
4. Personalise the release for the media
5. Follow the ten-step guide to professional press release layout
6. Build your reputation with key messages

To answer the WHY? questions, try and get a quote from a judge or an awarding organisation spokesperson.

When developing the rest of your release with answers to the WHY? question, bring out aspects of your company, its product or service that make it different.

Make sure the last sentence of the release contains your sales enquiry contact details.

Keep releases down to a few short sentences (four or five is ideal). Further information can be included under 'background notes' on a separate sheet.

Include the awarding body's press office details if you believe them to be appropriate (see example).

Template 3. Winning an award

(Fill in the brackets and print on your letterhead under a large 'PRESS RELEASE' heading)

(DATE)

(HEADLINE)

(TOWN/AREA) – based (YOUR BUSINESS NAME) was today named the (UK's) top company in (WHATEVER THE AWARD IS FOR). (YOUR BUSINESS NAME) beat off (NUMBER) competitors to win the prestigious (NAME OF AWARD).

JUDGING THE AWARDS, (AWARD JUDGE'S NAME) said: "(QUOTE)."

(LIST OF YOUR COMPANY'S UNIQUE FEATURES)

('HOW DO I GET IT?' DETAILS)

ENDS

For further details contact:
(YOUR NAME) at (YOUR DAY AND EVENING TELEPHONE DETAILS, PLUS MOBILE OR PAGER NUMBERS AND E-MAIL)

(AWARD PRESS OFFICE CONTACT DETAILS)

(EXAMPLE 3: WINNING AN AWARD PRESS RELEASE: 199 words)

XYZ Company

XYZ House, Any street, Any town, Any Post or Zip Code.
Any telephone , fax and e-mail numbers and details

PRESS RELEASE

20 January 1999

Welsh winner scoops top UK agricultural science prize

Cardiff-based XYZ Bio-research Company was today named winner of the prestigious ABC Agriculture Award, the 'Nobel' prize of British agricultural science. The award was made for their pioneering work on the early detection of JGE disease in sheep. As JGE is only treatable in its early stages, when it is difficult to detect, this could save British farmers millions of pounds.

ABC Award judge John Brown, president of the Agriculture Research Confederation said: "XYZ are a tremendous example of leading edge bio-research."

A spin-off from the United University of Wales' bio-research department, XYZ was set up two years ago by three scientists. Their aim is to find commercial applications for bio-research discoveries.

To date, XYZ have pioneered a potential cure for spontaneous abortions in pigs.

Contact the company on 0123 445678 for further details.

ENDS

For further details contact:

Joe Bloggs, Jessie Smith or Jim Brown, XYZ's research team members direct on 0123 445678 (day); or 9876 54321 (Joe Bloggs, evening); on 0321 321321 (Joe Bloggs' mobile); or Jim Smith, press officer, ABC Agriculture Award on 0234 555555 (day) or 0123 98765, pager number 333 444 555

(Technical notes enclosed)

4. New appointments

Notes

Recruiting new people to prominent positions, or promoting employees, shows your company is growing. That is a message worth getting across.

Press coverage of a new appointment is a quick and effective way of introducing a new member of staff to people. It is also a good idea to tell important customers about the appointment before it appears in the press.

The appointment release should show previous career highlights of your recruit. If the newcomer is a member of the management team, enclose a professionally-taken head and shoulders photograph.

Do not forget to send out a release if you are appointed to a professional association or trade body.

Remember to follow the Six Golden Rules on pages 117 to 127:

1. Use success words
2. Wrap up as many 5W Questions as you can in the first sentence (WHO? WHERE? WHAT? WHEN? WHY? – see case study examples on page 120)
3. Strip out the superlatives
4. Personalise the release for the media
5. Follow the ten-step guide to professional press release layout
6. Build your reputation with key messages

Appointment announcements appear in the press as one or two sentences, so do not make busy journalists edit your text. Keep appointment releases to the minimum.

Note that the sample provided gives you the excuse to distribute the release to the local press in your area, and also to the area where the new recruit comes from.

Template 4: New appointments

(Fill in the brackets and print on your letterhead under a large 'PRESS RELEASE' heading)

(DATE)

(HEADLINE)

(NAME) (AGE) was today appointed (JOB TITLE) of (TOWN/AREA) – based (YOUR BUSINESS NAME). He was previously (PREVIOUS JOB TITLE)

ENDS

For further details contact:
(YOUR NAME) at (YOUR DAY AND EVENING TELEPHONE DETAILS, PLUS ANY MOBILE OR PAGER NUMBERS AND E-MAIL)

(EXAMPLE 4: APPOINTMENT PRESS RELEASE: 94 words)

XYZ Company

XYZ House
Any street,
Any town,
any Post or Zip Code.
Any telephone and fax numbers
E-mail address

PRESS RELEASE

20 January 1999

Glasgow man gets top sales job at Cheshire packaging firm

Glasgow-born John Smith (29) was today named sales director of Cheshire-based packaging firm, the XYZ Company. Mr Smith was previously head of sales for ABC Ltd.

His appointment will spearhead a new sales drive for XYZ's unique range of impact-resistant packaging in Scotland and the rest of the UK.

XYZ Company is Britain's leading impact-resistant packaging specialists.

ENDS

For further details contact:
John Smith direct on 0123 445678 (day); on 9876 54321 (evening); or on 0321 321321 (mobile)

(Photo enclosed)

5. Anniversaries

Notes

Anniversaries show you have staying power. And in today's changing world, that deserves a press release.

If your business has some history, and the birthday is a big one, try and organize an event relating to the year you were founded.

Maybe one of the founders could be quoted?

If prices have fallen in real terms since you started, you could use the occasion to make that point. Or you could say that, due to increased efficiency, prices have gone up by X per cent since you were founded, compared to Y per cent on the Retail Price Index.

Anniversaries can be celebrated with an open day or party for customers and neighbours. Such occasions can be good photo opportunities (see Publishable Pictures on page 180).

The release should follow the Six Golden Rules on pages 117 to 127:

1. Use success words
2. Wrap up as many 5W Questions as you can in the first sentence (WHO? WHERE? WHAT? WHEN? WHY? – see case study examples on page 120)
3. Strip out the superlatives
4. Personalise the release for the media
5. Follow the ten-step guide to professional press release layout
6. Build your reputation with key messages

You can include a short list of the company's achievements in this sort of release: Firsts, innovative products, breakthroughs, etc.

The last sentence of the release should name the company's sales contact using a first name rather than initials.

Keep releases down to a few short sentences (four or five is ideal).

Further information can be included on a separate sheet headed 'Background Notes'.

Template 5. Anniversaries press release

(Fill in the brackets and print on your letterhead under a large 'PRESS RELEASE' heading)

(DATE)

(HEADLINE)

(TOWN/AREA) – based (YOUR BUSINESS NAME) will be celebrating its Xth anniversary on (DATE). To mark the occasion, the company will be (WHATEVER YOU PLAN TO DO).

Since the launch, (YOUR BUSINESS NAME) has (LIST MAIN ACHIEVEMENTS)

(QUOTE)

(SALES CONTACT DETAILS)

ENDS

For further details contact:
(YOUR NAME) at (YOUR DAY AND EVENING TELEPHONE DETAILS, PLUS ANY MOBILE OR PAGER NUMBERS AND E-MAIL)

(Company history details enclosed)

(EXAMPLE 5: ANNIVERSARIES PRESS RELEASE: 200 words)

XYZ Company

XYZ House, Any street, Any town, Any Post or Zip Code.
Any telephone and fax numbers. E-mail address

PRESS RELEASE

20 January 1999

Portsmouth pottery raffles manor house away in 10th birthday celebrations

Portsmouth-based pottery, XYZ will be celebrating its 10th birthday next week with a free raffle to win the Manor House, a 12" ceramic sculpture worth £350, from XYZ's award-winning UK domestic architecture series. Five other winners will receive their choice from the 'miniature cottage' series. All visitors to the shop can enter the draw.

XYZ was set up by husband and wife team John and Jean Smith after John was made redundant. It now employs five people and sends its ceramic sculptures all over the world.

XYZ is best known for popular limited editions of traditional domestic buildings, sought by collectors in many countries. Its high standard of craftsmanship has been recognised by numerous awards.

XYZ Pottery is at 123 High Street.

ENDS

For further details contact:
John or Jean Smith on 0123 445678 (day) or 9876 54321 (evening)

PHOTOCALL INVITATION
Councillor's daughter draws prize raffle
The raffle will be drawn at noon on 27th January by local councillor Joe Bloggs and his daughter Jessica (eight). You are welcome to send a photographer to XYZ, 123 High Street, Portsmouth where the Manor House will be on display.

(Company history details attached.)

6. Business expansion

Notes

Taking on new staff or building an extension is expansion of the business. Any business expansion sends out a positive signal that is certainly worth amplifying.

- Are you expanding premises?
- Expanding your production team?
- Expanding your sales team?
- Expanding into new markets: industrial, business or commercial sectors?
- New geographic areas?
- Expanding your range of products or services?

If a new building is involved, you can have a press release at each phase:

1. Announce the project is going ahead
2. Have a 'ground-breaking' or 'turning the sod' photocall
3. Arrange a topping-out ceremony, with photocall, when the roof's on
4. Organize a grand opening, again with a photocall.

Highlight staff increases: new jobs in any area are important.

Remember to follow the Six Golden Rules on pages 117 to 127:
1. Use success words
2. Wrap up as many 5W Questions as you can in the first sentence (WHO? WHERE? WHAT? WHEN? WHY? – see case study examples on page 120)
3. Strip out the superlatives
4. Personalise the release for the media
5. Follow the ten-step guide to professional press release layout on pages 125-6
6. Build your reputation with key messages

Answers to the WHY? question are often best addressed in the second and third sentences.

If the business expansion is associated with new business wins, remember the power of third party endorsement. See if you can answer the WHY? question with a quote from the customer:

WHY do they buy your products or service?

WHY have they appointed you as a dealer, licensee or franchisee?

When developing the rest of your release with answers to the WHY? question, bring out aspects of your product or service that make it different from the others.

- Why is it different?
- Why is it better?
- Why is it new?
- Why is it innovative?
- What gives it that extra spark?

The last sentence of the release should wrap up the 'How do I get it?' details: price, where it can be bought or whom to contact for sales.

Keep releases down to a few short sentences (four or five is ideal). Further information can be included on a separate 'Background Notes' sheet. This gives the journal a choice to include additional information from these notes rather than you trying to cram everything into the text of the release.

Template 6. Business expansion

(Fill in the brackets and print on your letterhead under a large 'PRESS RELEASE' heading)

(DATE)

(HEADLINE)

(TOWN/AREA) – based (YOUR BUSINESS NAME) today announced an additional (TYPE OF EXPANSION) for its (PRODUCTS) at the (PLACE). The additional facilities will result in (WHAT?: STAFF INCREASES? EXTRA PRODUCTION CAPABILITY? INCREASED TURNOVER?). Work on the new facility scheduled to commence on (DATE), will open (WHEN?)

(YOUR CUSTOMER'S PERSON AND JOB TITLE) said: "(QUOTE)".

(LIST UNIQUE DETAILS OF YOUR PRODUCT OR SERVICE)

(YOUR KEY MESSAGE)

('HOW DO I GET IT?' DETAILS)

ENDS

For further details contact:
(YOUR NAME) at (YOUR DAY AND EVENING TELEPHONE DETAILS, PLUS ANY MOBILE OR PAGER NUMBERS AND E-MAIL)

(CLIENT PRESS CONTACT AND CONTACT DETAILS)

(Offer photos "available on request" if you have them.)

(EXAMPLE 6: BUSINESS EXPANSION: 200 words)

XYZ Company

XYZ House, Any street, Any town, Any Post or Zip Code.
Any telephone and fax numbers and e-mail addresses

PRESS RELEASE

20 January 1999

Washington firm to expand

Washington-based top millenary firm XYZ Company today announced they are to build an additional manufacturing facility in Any Street, Washington. Thanks to an increase in orders from London-based fashion houses, they plan to double the workforce.

Julie Bloggs, who started XYZ eight years ago from her Washington home, said: "Curt Pretzel, the famous international designer, saw one of our special hats at a wedding and asked to see more. Since then, headpieces have been featured in his fashion shows and the word is spreading."

XYZ moved into an old mill on Any Street five years ago. They have commissioned a purpose-built production unit on an adjacent site. They will keep their administration staff in the old mill and let out the top two floors as offices.

Work on the new project is scheduled to begin on 15th February; the new facility will open six months later.

XYZ specialise in one-off custom-made hats for special occasions, with prices starting at £75 ($100). For more information, contact Julie Bloggs on 0123 445566.

ENDS

For further details contact:
Julie Bloggs direct on 0123 445566 (day) or 9876 54321 (evening); or page her on 0123 98765, pager number 333 444 555

PRESS PHOTOGRAPHS AVAILABLE ON REQUEST

7. Surveys

Notes

Surveys are one of the best ways of generating publicity. Subject matter can be anything you could reasonably be expected to know about in your business area.

For example, different angles on the effects of stress could be surveyed by management consultants, lawyers, organisational change consultants, psychologists, health farms and almost anyone connected to the health business, both mainstream and alternative.

Survey tips

Think of subjects that have a wide appeal for popular press coverage:

- diets
- health
- work
- money
- human relationships
- home
- family
- holidays
- cars
- pets

Then build up your survey questions.

Keep the surveys simple and easy to handle: two to five questions is ample, with easy to answer categories.

To see how the questions and answers work, first try them out on a few people.

For maximum effect, release survey data when things are quiet:

- on a Sunday for Monday's papers
- during the July holiday period
- between Christmas and New Year.

The release should follow the Six Golden Rules on pages 117 to 127:

1. Use success words
2. Wrap up as many 5W Questions as you can in the first sentence (WHO? WHERE? WHAT? WHEN? WHY? – See case study examples on page 120)
3. Strip out the superlatives
4. Personalise the release for the media
5. Follow the ten-step guide to professional press release layout
6. Build your reputation with key messages

Keep survey releases down to a few short sentences (four or five is ideal), bringing out the highlights. Enclose a copy of the full survey with the release and be prepared to fax key parts of your data on request.

Template 7. Surveys

(Fill in the brackets and print on your letterhead under a large 'PRESS RELEASE' heading)

(DATE)

(HEADLINE)

(KEY SURVEY FINDING) was revealed today by a survey conducted by (TOWN/AREA) – based (YOUR BUSINESS NAME AND TYPE OF BUSINESS). The survey, which polled (WHAT CATEGORY OF PEOPLE?), also found:

(LIST OTHER KEY FINDINGS: HIGHLIGHTS)
Commenting on the survey results, (YOUR NAME AND JOB TITLE) of XYZ said: (QUOTE)

(YOUR KEY MESSAGE)

('HOW DO I GET IT?' DETAILS)

ENDS

For further details contact:
(YOUR NAME) at (YOUR DAY AND EVENING TELEPHONE DETAILS, PLUS ANY MOBILE OR PAGER NUMBERS AND E-MAIL)

(ENCLOSE SURVEY DATA OR SAY THAT FULL SURVEY DETAILS ARE AVAILABLE ON REQUEST)

(EXAMPLE 7: SURVEY: 196 words)

XYZ Company

XYZ House, Any street, Any town, Any Post or Zip Code.
Any telephone and fax numbers and your E-mail address

PRESS RELEASE

20 January 1999

Norwich survey reveals dogs are man's best friend

A survey conducted by Norwich-based XYZ pet shop reveals that 62 per cent of its male customers prefer their dogs to humans. Results announced today show only three per cent of female customers rated their dogs more highly than human friends.

The survey, conducted among XYZ customers over a three-month period, also revealed that pet owners were more likely to take out health insurance for their pets than for themselves. XYZ is an agent for ABC Pet Insurance.

XYZ owner Joe Bloggs said: "We knew that dog owners have a special bond with their pets. But we had no idea the survey would reveal that 'man's best friend is his dog' would turn out to be quite literally true."

XYZ opened their petstore in Norwich three years ago with the aim of being the number one petcare centre in Norwich. In addition to a wide range of pet foods, books and accessories, they run a pet-grooming service and discounted Pet Health Insurance.

XYZ is at 123 Anystreet, Norwich.

ENDS

For further details contact:
Joe Bloggs on 0123 445566 (day) or 9876 54321 (evening)

Dog owners survey by XYZ
Survey results

Q1: Would you rather spend time with your dog than human companions?

Male responses:

Yes	62%
No	28%
No opinion	10%

Female responses:

Yes	3%
No	91%
No opinion:	6%

Q2: Do you have private health insurance:

For yourself?
For your dog?

Male responses:

Yes – For yourself:	13%
Yes – For your dog:	15%

Female responses:

Yes – For yourself:	15%
Yes – For your dog:	18%

8. Issues

Notes

Find a topical issue that is already attracting press comment or some controversy that is relevant to your business. Then put out a press release commenting on the issue, as long as you have a reasonable reason for expressing your views. The issue can be local, national or international.

Threats to a business or industry are a credible reason to state your views. A by-pass which may affect your petrol station business would generate publicity in the local press. You may not be able to stop the event but they may agree to signpost your station.

Similarly, the local press may be interested in your views on how a proposed out-of-town shopping centre will hit your business. New traffic and parking restrictions hit retail businesses. Perhaps you can highlight the plight of a group of traders and get some concessions in the form of reduced business rates or a relaxation of the parking rules, or a free shoppers' bus?

If the threat is more general, you may get wider publicity in the regional or national press. You may be a threatened industry calling for more regional aid. If you could be put out of business by Euro legislation, you could get national coverage. The campaign to exempt the great British banger from EC regulations on sausages is a good example.

If you can make your comments in public, perhaps as the speaker at a trade association or business club dinner, you have extra credibility.

If you do use a public speech as a platform to raise an issue and generate press comment, make sure you have copies of your speech available in case the press ask for one. Make sure your release goes out in advance of, or at the same time as, your speech.

TEN PRESS RELEASE TEMPLATES

When you become better known as a spokesperson on your chosen issue, you will be able to ring up key journalists and tell them of the specific points you will be making during a speech that day.

The release should follow the Six Golden Rules on pages 117 to 127:

1.   Use success words
2.   Wrap up as many 5W Questions as you can in the first sentence (WHO? WHERE? WHAT? WHEN? WHY? – see case study examples on page 120)
3.   Strip out the superlatives
4.   Personalise the release for the media
5.   Follow the ten-step guide to professional press release layout
6.   Build your reputation with key messages

Keep releases down to a few short sentences (four or five is ideal).

Template 8. Issues

(Fill in the brackets and print on your letterhead under a large 'PRESS RELEASE' heading)

(DATE)

(HEADLINE: SOUND A WARNING)

(YOUR NAME AND JOB TITLE) of (PLACE)-based XYZ warned against (KEY ISSUE) today at a meeting of the (NAME OR ORGANISATION YOU WERE ADDRESSING)

(LIST OTHER KEY POINTS BRIEFLY)

(YOUR KEY MESSAGE)

ENDS

For further details contact:
(YOUR NAME) at (YOUR DAY AND EVENING TELEPHONE DETAILS, PLUS ANY MOBILE OR PAGER NUMBERS AND E-MAIL)

(EXAMPLE 8: ISSUES: 195 words)

XYZ Company

XYZ House, Any street, Any town, Any Post or Zip Code.
Any telephone and fax numbers and E-mail address

PRESS RELEASE

20 January 1999

Maidenhead management consultants sound stress warning

Employers are ignoring the dangers of stress at work, according to Maidenhead-based management consultants XYZ. Joe Bloggs, XYZ's expert in stress in employment, says "Almost all the companies we see have no provision for measuring stress levels at work, despite the recent six-figure landmark court awards for stressed employees."

XYZ's findings are in line with recent research carried out by the ABC Institute showing nine out of ten companies were taking no steps to avoid potentially-damaging legal actions raised by stressed staff.

XYZ launched its unique stress monitor system a few months ago, based on leading edge research conducted at the University of ABC's psychology department. The stress monitor highlights potential risk areas through a series of self-assessment questionnaires and follow-up interviews. A confidential report highlights individuals at most risk and contains straightforward recommendations to improve the situation. A six-month follow-up checks the implementation of recommendations.

For further details of the stress monitor check from XYZ, ring Joe Bloggs on 0123 456789.

ENDS

For further details contact:
Joe Bloggs on 0123 456789 (day) or 9876 54321 (evening)

9. Charities and sponsorship

Notes

Involvement with a charity or a sponsorship is not just about making cash donations. Your support can take many forms: participation on the board, or assistance with an event or providing goods and services (known as 'sponsorship in kind'). If you have a retail outlet, perhaps you could arrange an associated window display or act as a collection point for sponsorship forms? If you have computer expertise, you could help with collating the results of an event? All of which would be good reasons to issue a press release.

Charitable involvement will give you a higher profile, so choose a reputable charity.

Charity-related press release opportunities include announcing your involvement with a high profile fund-raising campaign or putting out a release about your appointment to the charity's board As with all co-operative ventures, seek clearance from the charity concerned before contacting the media: they may well offer to put out the release themselves and save you the effort.

Fund-raising lends itself to creative and wacky events. So be on the lookout for press photocall opportunities.

This is a case where the Six Golden Rules on pages 117 to 127 have to be applied with extra sensitivity. It would be inappropriate to over-commercialise your release; so content yourself with a mention and substitute the charity's own key messages.

1. Use success words
2. Wrap up as many 5W Questions as you can in the first sentence (WHO? WHERE? WHAT? WHEN? WHY? – See case study examples on page 120)

3. Strip out the superlatives
4. Personalise the release for the media
5. Follow the ten-step guide to professional press release layout on pages 125-6
6. Build your reputation with key messages

Bring in a quote if it contains further useful information.
Keep releases down to a few short sentences (four or five is ideal).

Template 9. Charities and sponsorship

(Fill in the brackets and print on your letterhead under a large 'PRESS RELEASE' heading)

(DATE)

(HEADLINE)

(PLACE)-based XYZ has joined up with (CHARITY NAME) and will be (WHATEVER YOUR INVOLVEMENT IS)

(QUOTE FROM CHARITY SPOKESPERSON)

(LIST THE KEY AIMS OF THE CHARITY INVOLVED)

(INCLUDE THE CHARITY'S KEY MESSAGES)

ENDS

For further details contact:
(YOUR NAME) at (YOUR DAY AND EVENING TELEPHONE DETAILS, PLUS MOBILE OR PAGER NUMBERS AND E-MAIL)

Or
(CHARITY PRESS CONTACT DETAILS)

(EXAMPLE 9: CHARITIES & SPONSORSHIP: 200 words)

XYZ Company

XYZ House, Any street, Any town, any Post or Zip Code.
Any telephone and fax numbers and E-mail address

PRESS RELEASE

20 January 1999

Brighton cleaning firm backs arthritis charity race

Brighton-based XYZ company is backing the local Arthritis Campaign's annual sponsored race on the prom, starting at 10am on Sunday, 11 April. XYZ are lending their offices, which overlook the finishing line, as race headquarters. They are providing computers and trained operators to help the organisers and will also host a 'thank you' tea for race stewards and officials. Prizes will be presented by Samantha Someone.

Joe Bloggs, managing director of XYZ said: "A number of our customers have arthritis. This is our way of giving something back."

Jim Smith, chairman of the Brighton and Hove branch of Arthritis Care, added: "We are delighted XYZ have offered such practical support."

The race is over three miles along a route verified by the Amateur Road Runners' Association. Money raised will be used for arthritis treatment research. Last year's race raised £33,000.

ENDS

For further details contact:
Joe Bloggs on 0123 445566 (day) or 9876 54321 (evening)

Or
Arthritis Campaign's press officer, Julie Smith, on 0217 999 9999(day) or page her on 0123 98765, pager 333 444 555

10. Competition success

Notes

Sporting or competition success implies bright, motivated and keen people. Just the sort of qualities you want to be publicly associated with your business. If you have a sporting or leisure passion that leads you to the prize-winner's table, or if any of your staff are hot competitors in anything from golf to flea circuses, make sure you put out a release about successes. Remember to mention their job title in the release.

Tee-shirts with your company's name are relatively inexpensive, but useful for prize-giving photographs.

The wackier the event, the more press appeal it has. So whether it's a scrambling champion or a top wellie whanger, let the press know.

Don't overdo the commercialism: this is a leisure pursuit we are celebrating. But do go for a company mention.

As always, the Six Golden Rules referred to on pages 117 to 127 will keep you on track:

1. Use success words
2. Wrap up as many 5W Questions as you can in the first sentence (WHO? WHERE? WHAT? WHEN? WHY? – See case study examples on page 120)
3. Strip out the superlatives
4. Personalise the release for the media
5. Follow the ten-step guide to professional press release layout
6. Build your reputation with key messages

Template 10. Competitions

(Fill in the brackets and print on your letterhead under a large 'PRESS RELEASE' heading)

(DATE)

(HEADLINE)

(WINNER'S NAME AND JOB TITLE) from (PLACE)-based XYZ has won a (COMPETITION AND PRIZE)

(QUOTE FROM COMPETITION ORGANISER)

(QUOTE FROM YOURSELF)

ENDS

For further details contact:
(YOUR NAME) at (YOUR DAY AND EVENING TELEPHONE DETAILS, PLUS MOBILE OR PAGER NUMBERS AND E-MAIL)

Or
(COMPETITION ORGANISER'S PRESS OFFICE CONTACT DETAILS)

(EXAMPLE 10: COMPETITIONS: 182 words)

XYZ Company

XYZ House, Any street, Any town, Any Post or Zip Code.
Any telephone and fax numbers and E-mail address

PRESS RELEASE

20 January 1999

Fulham nursing home team wins trivia challenge

A team of three from Fulham-based XYZ nursing home have won London's annual ABC Trivia Quiz, sponsored by ABC Breweries.

Jessie Smith, Julia Brown and Joan Black won through four heats involving teams from all over London. In a close-fought final at the Nag's Head in Some Street, they beat three other teams.

John Smith, the sponsor's marketing manager, said: "These ladies are a fund of information, worthy winners of the ABC Trivia trophy. They each win a week for two at ABCWorld Leisure Centre in Someshire."

Joe Bloggs, managing director of XYZ, said: "Our people are always helping residents to enter competitions. They're a lively bunch and I'm proud of them."

ENDS

For further details contact:
Joe Bloggs at XYZ Nursing Home on 0123 445566 (day) or 9876 54321 (evening)
Or
Joan Brown at ABC Breweries' Press Office on 0217 999 9999 (office); or pager 0123 98765, pager number 333444555

CHAPTER 9.

HANDLING PRESS INTERVIEWS

Journalists do their homework. They often have access to on-line electronic press cuttings research systems like Reuters Business Information System. They just key in your company's name and, within a few seconds, up on the screen comes up to ten years of press cuttings about your business. So, if you have been in the press, they will know about it.

The great advantage you have is that you probably know more about your subject than the journalist. If you get a chance to chat to the interviewer before a radio or TV recording, they will probably base their questions on that seemingly casual chat.

Make sure you get your key points across and don't get lured into saying anything you would not want to be broadcast or see in print. No matter what the journalist says: it's your word against his that you were speaking 'off the record'. Once that damage is done, it is very difficult to repair.

Even when the notebook or recorder is put away, don't assume you can say anything you like; the interviewer will not hesitate to memorise an incautious remark if it makes for a better story.

If journalists or broadcasters have not had time to do their homework, they will approach the interview by asking the five Ws: Who? What?

HANDLING PRESS INTERVIEWS

Where? When? and Why? For example:

■ Who are you? Who is behind your company? Who are your customers?
■ What does your business do? What part do you play?
■ Where is your business based? Where are your customers? Where did the incident happen (if indeed there is an incident)?
■ When did you set up the business? When did whatever it is they want to talk about occur?
■ Why did you set up the business? Why did it happen (if, indeed, anything did happen)?

So that you are prepared, it's a good idea to work out, in advance, what they are likely to ask and what your best response is. Don't make it a lengthy response. Unless it's an in-depth profile of you and your business, assume you will be lucky to get three short sentences in once the interview has been edited. Get your main points down to three short, pithy comments. If it's TV or radio, make sure they sound all right, then memorise them. You will sound stilted if you read a prepared statement.

When you are asked to do an interview

Unless you have already done a number of interviews on the same topic, you cannot possibly work out appropriate response off the top of your head. So don't leap straight in when the interview is requested. They will probably ask if you can say a few words over the telephone. If it's radio, that probably means they have started recording.

Stall them to give yourself five to ten minutes to sort out your response. Say "Yes, I'd love to comment, but can I call back in five minutes when I've finished this meeting? Can I just take a few details of what you want?"

Or, "Yes, I'll be right back to you, but I just want to check the latest state of play. Can I ring you in ten minutes? Can I just check what you want?"

Then, before you ring off, ask the following questions.

Interview checklist:

When you are asked for an interview, write down the answers to these questions. Unless you do, you will kick yourself later.

- What is your name?
- What is your number?
- Which radio/TV station/magazine/newspaper did you say you were from?
- (Radio/TV only) What is the programme?
- (Radio/TV only) When is it going out?
- (Radio/TV only) Is it live or pre-recorded?
- Is anyone else is being interviewed on the subject for this programme?
- What sort of line are you taking? (They will not commit themselves to asking specific questions because they will respond to whatever you say).

Sort out your three points and *ring back when you said you would.*

If you are going to do the interview in a radio studio, take along a spare cassette tape and ask if you can have a copy; they are not meant to do it, but most will. If it's an interview down the telephone line, or a TV interview, you will have to organize your own recording.

Getting your point across

- Decide three short points in advance
- Keep them short and pithy
- Make sure you get your points across

HANDLING PRESS INTERVIEWS

While you may be in the media eye for a positive achievement, it's the negative situations that are harder to handle.

If you are handling something tricky say, for example, a possibility that you have polluted the environment, your lawyers may be involved. The name of the game is not denial, but damage limitation. You will need to agree a carefully-worded statement confirming what the position is and what you are doing about it. Stick to that politely and refuse to be drawn further. Phrases like "We're still looking into that" are useful.

As thoughts of potential lawsuits fill your head, the temptation is to panic. Don't retreat into the 'no comment' situation that lawyers often advise. It looks suspicious. Develop a prepared press statement with your legal advisers. To refuse to comment looks like an admission of guilt, which is why a statement is necessary.

Watch out for the long pause: it's probably an interviewers' trick. It is all too easy to leap in and say something to fill the silence, especially if you are nervous.

No-one expects you to wave a magic wand and make a complicated problem disappear. Nor do they expect you to admit guilt if there is reasonable doubt as to what has happened. It also helps if you are an award-winning company that is proven itself to be environmentally aware, as long as you make sure that the media knows about it.

Keep your cool and remain polite, even if you think the interviewer is being unfair. It's counter-productive to take issue vehemently, especially on radio or TV. Remember that the interviewer is the voice or face that is familiar. The audience believes the interviewer is on their side. If they did not, ratings would drop and the interviewer would be replaced.

Case study:
The butcher in the E-Coli trap

You do not need to be an industrial giant to be caught in the middle of a high profile incident. A Scottish butcher's shop in a small town was at the centre of one of the worst public health incidents in the country. Several people died from eating infected meat apparently supplied by the shop.

The media handling of the incident reflected the fact that they were dealing with a relatively small business. In comparison to the way they handle larger concerns, they did not adopt a particularly aggressive stance.

The butcher in question had won nationally-recognised awards; the shop's recognition was faithfully reported throughout the early reporting stages.

To the outside observer, that award-winning status established a sense that the business was committed to excellence. The impression given by TV reports was that, if it happened to them, it could happen to any butcher.

Even when the situation got worse and the firm did retreat behind their lawyers, that earlier reporting must have stood them in good stead.

I don't know whether or not that the shop had PR advisers. But the reporting of those awards plus their obviously good customer relations, probably saved the business. I saw TV interviews with customers who spoke with glowing praise about the butcher's products and service.

The shop went through a rough time but it was eventually able to re-open. Had the shop looked run-down. If it had not won an award. If it had just given a barely adequate service to customers, it would not have survived.

It's always difficult when you are in the middle of an incident to feel you are being fairly treated. The media do use emotive language but it's not personal. They treat everyone the same, so you have to take headlines like 'Bungles, mistakes and excuses' with a pinch of salt.

If you can provide the counterbalance: "Yes, we boobed, but we've fixed it, and amended our systems so it's much less likely to happen again", most journalists will give you the benefit of the doubt – unless they have already caught you lying to them. Honesty is the best policy when dealing with the media, but that does not mean offering negative information. Play to your strengths.

What to say in a spot

Phrases that show you are concerned and doing everything you can to assess and sort out the situation are what is required. However, your comments must be based on the truth or you will be crucified by the media. "We've got experts looking into that and they tell us it's too early to say" are fine if you really do have a credible expert looking into it.

Similarly, if you have an environmental policy and a good track record, make sure you get that across. "We're proud of our green record. We won an award last year for our environmental processes. So you can imagine how seriously we take these pollution allegations." (Note how you are already turning accusations into the shifting sands of 'allegation'.) "We're doing everything we can to assess things. It's too early to tell whether we're the source (Note: you introduce an element of doubt that you are the only possible source) but we'll be conducting a full enquiry."

Some people may feel that these are 'weasel word' tactics, twisting the truth to your advantage but in the early stages of most problems, no-one knows what the truth is. In the world of TV and tabloid journalism, no-one will be holding back in the accusation department. If there is room to introduce doubt, use it.

TOP TIP: If you are being interviewed on the telephone for radio, make sure the background is quiet. If you are in the studio, remove from your pockets anything that might rattle; and don't fidget near the microphone.

TV Techniques

Everything said above applies here, but there is an important additional visual element. People remember visuals long after the words are gone, so make sure you look the part.

Practice keeping your head and eyes steady, looking straight into the camera or at the interviewer. (Ask where to look).

If you are asked to go into a TV studio, be prepared to enter an alien environment where there is a lot happening. Make sure you are comfortable, preferably wearing pastels or medium colours. Very bright or very dark colours can throw some camera exposure systems. Unless you avoid large amounts of solid black, dark navy or pure white, your skin tone may look a little odd on camera.

HANDLING PRESS INTERVIEWS

Another choice to avoid is bright checks, strong patterns or tweeds, which can cause the camera to produce a disconcerting flickering effect called strobing.

If you cannot stand bright light when you wear contact lenses, leave them out: I know a senior executive who wished he had. Normally a fluent and articulate spokesman, he was never asked back into one TV station after doing a three-minute interview with tears pouring down his cheeks. A crying man does not make for good business TV – unless, of course, there's major economic crisis.

If you are offered make-up, accept it, even if you are a man. TV people know their studio set-up. If they offer make-up, it's nothing personal. It's because the studio lights are so bright that you will look unnaturally death-like without some artificial help. Fortunately, cameras are much better than they used to be.

Of course TV interviews are not always in the studio. TV news interviews are often short 'sound-bites' lasting fifteen to thirty seconds. Sound-bites are often filmed in front of a relevant building or business process in operation by a mobile outside broadcast unit (OBU). An OBU consists of a camera operator, sound recording technician and the interviewer. The trend is slowly moving towards interviewers handling light video cameras themselves; some cable and community TV channels already operate in this way.

CHAPTER 10.

PRESS PHOTOS AND TV VISUALS

Photos and the press

Virtually all publications need professional quality photographs but there is a difference in the way trade magazines and newspapers treat photos for publication.

Daily newspapers

Most daily newspapers have a picture editor and their own team of photographers, backed up by freelance press photographers all over the country. These photographers know what the picture editor wants; it is their job to go out and get the kind of pictures he or she prefers.

To get these photographers to come to your event, you need to persuade the picture desk that you are offering a dramatically visual photo opportunity. Study the type of photos used by various papers. Then try to arrange a strongly visual event.

Send out an invitation, addressed to the picture desk, describing the visual aspect of your photo opportunity and the people who will be there. When you are dealing with daily newspapers, this invitation should be separate from any press release because the picture desk and news desks are separate departments.

PRESS PHOTOS AND TV VISUALS

Weekly newspapers

Because weekly newspapers often have limited photographic resources, it's sometimes worth submitting photos taken by professional press photographers – if the budget allows.

Business magazines

High-quality national business magazines will, in most cases, confine themselves to photography they have commissioned. However, regional and local business magazines often rely on submitted photos.

Trade magazines

Many trade magazines will carry photos submitted for publication, but watch out for colour separation fees for printing your photo. These fees are usually disguised advertising charges.

Sample Press Photocall Invitation to newspaper picture desks

PHOTOCALL... PHOTOCALL... PHOTOCALL... PHOTOCALL...

1 February 1999

On 9 February at 10am in the Internet Cyber Cafe, 14 Anystreet, Anytown: 12 children will be tangled up in a giant net web with adults, as they show their parents how to surf the net.

The giant web event marks the launch of XYZ's new website, designed to sell XYZ's unique on-line training solutions to the English-speaking world.

ENDS

For further details, contact Joe Bloggs on 1234 56789 (day or evening)

Six steps to running smooth photocalls

1. Phone round the picture desks a couple of days before the event to check they received the invitation and ask whether your photocall 'has made the diary'. If it has, that is as good as you will get. It means you are in with a chance; the rest is down to whatever competition there is on the day for attractive picture opportunities.

2. On the day, make sure that you or someone who knows a lot about the event, arrives half an hour early and is prepared to stay for a couple of hours to greet the press.

3. Be prepared for disappointment. Press photographers go from unpredictable assignment to assignment, and picture editors amend their schedule as hard news stories break. Even firm promises from media friends can crumble in the face of a major news picture opportunity. All you can do is hope.

4. Press photographers often run late, so you will need to ensure the key subject of your photocall is available for as long as possible.

5. Make sure you have a press release giving details of the event. It's important to include names and job titles of key people. Double check the spelling of names. No-one likes to see their name spelt wrongly in publications.

6. Write down the names of the photographers, and the papers they are covering, so you can buy the papers to check results. Find out whether they are freelance or staff photographers, so that you can identify good freelance people should you need to commission press shots in your area.

TOP TIP: Monday's papers are often short of good photos, so arrange your photocall on a Sunday, when many PR professionals are week-ending.

PRESS PHOTOS AND TV VISUALS

If your heart's set on getting into the Sunday papers, a photocall late on Friday would have more chance than earlier in the week.

REPUTATION SAVER: Never send photocall invitations or pictures to a radio station.

Commissioning press photographers

Daily papers very rarely used submitted material. That is why there is little point in paying a professional photographer to take pictures for submission 'on spec' to the dailies.

The exception is a freelance photographer currently being used regularly (at least once a week) by your most important target daily paper. In this case, the photographer would be in a good position to get a photograph relating to your business on to the picture editor's desk.

Remember, there is no guarantee of success, so do not shell out money you can ill afford. However, if you need the photos for any other reason, you might as well order a few more press prints.

Good quality material is required by magazines and the weekly press. That means finding a good freelance press photographer.

Finding good press photographers
Press photographers are different from the photographer in the High Street studio. Press photographers have developed super-fast reflexes to get just the right photo out of a changing event. Studio photographers are used to a set, controlled environment. They can be used for portraits and brochure pictures, but do not hire them to cover an event.

If you want to identify freelance press photographers (as opposed to 'ordinary' photographers) find out who the press are currently using. You can try ringing newspaper photo departments and asking whether they use a freelance photographer in your area. Alternatively, source them through the National Union of Journalists (see information section on page 201).

Ten tips for commissioning freelance press photographers

1. When you commission a press photographer, describe the situation or event in detail.

2. Ask for their ideas to make a press picture out of the situation you have described.

3. Get an estimate in advance. Charges are usually by the hour plus travel, materials (film, processing and prints). If your budget is limited, set a maximum price for the job, including proofs and a specified number of prints or transparencies.

4. Ask how much extra prints will cost.

5. Ask about copyright restrictions.

6. Tell them whether you want prints (and the size of print you want) or transparencies.

7. Black and white or colour.

8. Tell them if you need several different photos for different publications.

9. If the photographer is supplying photographic prints, ask whether they offer machine proof prints (ordinary 5x3" sized prints) or colour contact proofs (little reference prints of the whole film all on the same sheet). You cannot get proofs of any type if the photographer is using transparency film.

10. Find out how long it will take to get the proofs, and how long for final prints.

Publishable pictures

Publishable pictures are those that are of good quality and dramatic visual impact.

Subject matter should dominate the picture; the photographer should have dramatised the photo with the use of visual props or a dramatic angle. The picture should have strong visual appeal. The standard 'grip and grin' of two people shaking hands is a real turn-off to most picture editors, as are pictures of people standing apart from each other. Bunch people up tightly for better photos.

It's essential that photos are free of faults and blemishes. They must also be free of copyright restrictions.

Make sure you submit the right type of photo to the press: black and white or colour, depending on the needs of the publication in question.

Ten rules for submitting photos for publication

1. Photographs must be transparencies (see box on page 182) or prints made from original negatives to which you have copyright clearance. Photographic copyright in the UK usually rests with the photographer, unless they have assigned their rights to someone else. This is true even if you have commissioned them.

2. It's technically and legally impossible for the press to reproduce photographs that have been cut out of a printed publication, even your own brochure.

3. Photographic prints should be at least 7in x 5in and preferably 8in x 6in or 10in x 8in.

4. All photographs should be in focus, with the subject matter dominating the picture.

5. Photographic prints must be free of folds, creases or blemishes. Never use paper clips or staples to attach anything to a photo. If you have to post it, always protect the photo with card.

6. Never write on the back of photographic prints: the indents will show through. Captions should be attached to the back of photographic prints, with sticky tape.

7. Transparencies are sometimes supplied in strips with a clear plastic cover. They can also be mounted in card or glass mounts to protect the film. Do not post glass-mounted slides; you risk smashing and damaging them.

8. Do not send original transparencies: they cannot be replaced. Get transparencies duplicated at photo processing labs (see *Yellow Pages*).

9. Always write captions giving the name of the event, your company name and the names (check spelling) and job titles of people in the photo. Attach the caption with sticky tape to the back of a print, on to the slide mount or the clear plastic protective cover. Never tape direct on to the front of a print or onto any part of a transparency.

10. Do not expect your photos to be returned, even if the publication promises to do so. With the best will in the world, photos get lost in busy offices, or between the publisher and the reproduction house.

Colour transparencies or 'slides'

Colour transparencies (or 'slides') are colour photos taken with colour transparency film. A transparency is the actual piece of film after processing. It cannot be replaced, so handle with care.

You can tell the difference between a transparency or negative very easily. A colour negative is on orange film, and the colours are the opposite of what they are supposed to be. A transparency is on clear film and the colours look correct.

Publications used to insist on colour transparencies, but all that is changed due to modern scanning technology. Colour prints are now usually preferred. You can get colour prints made cheaply from negatives but it's very expensive to get prints made from transparencies at a photo lab (see *Yellow Pages*).

Getting the TV cameras in

It's exciting when you attract TV cameras to your events. You can reach an astonishing number of people in a very short time. However, it's not easy to attract cameras as there are a limited number of Outside Broadcast crews per TV station.

Sometimes the quirky can get results if you just happen to be in the right place at the right time. For instance, a new teddy ward for a doll's hospital would stand a better chance of generating local TV coverage than yet another boring prize presentation (depending on who is presenting the prize). The teddy ward could make a neat "And finally" endpiece to a regional news bulletin.

Do not forget to include cable TV in your press list research.

Five ways to maximise TV coverage

- First of all, it helps if your idea is visual and topical.
- Second, try and ride on the back of another event that is likely to attract TV attention: a major football club's stormy annual general meeting, a conference or other major event.
- Thirdly, try to make it hard to edit out your company name: Tee-shirts or umbrellas with your name and logo are handy.
- Fourthly: you must have luck on your side. The best, most topical and visual TV opportunities will not attract TV crews if a 'hard' news story unfolds a few miles away. You are out of luck if (heaven forbid) there is a 60-car pile-up, an armed siege, or prison riot.
- Finally, patience brings its rewards. If you have enough strong visual ideas linked to topical themes, you will eventually make it. But even then, they may not give your company a mention. It costs a lot to broadcast every second and if you are not paying for it, you do not have any rights.

Be visually creative, but do not put all your eggs in one basket or spend a lot of money on something that may never happen.

GOING INTO PRINT

Press relations is great publicity but sometimes you wish you had more control over what was said, or more space in which to say it. It does cost money to produce a decent newsletter, but it's much cheaper than a glossy brochure and you can send it out regularly, keeping customers and potential customers up-to-date about your products or services. Because most of the costs involved in a publication are up-front, the bigger the distribution list, the more cost-effective a publication becomes.

A newsletter gives you a tangible mailshot opportunity and you can include the press in the distribution. It allows you to demonstrate your expertise in action and regularly gets stories in front of your target audience. If the publication is genuinely useful to busy recipients, with lots of bullets and checklists, it will be kept for reference.

Because people tend to trust the familiar, a regular newsletter will build up familiarity with your name. As a PR tool it will give you the name awareness and credibility that will facilitate *but not replace* your sales effort.

Ideally, a newsletter should be quarterly. They have a cumulative effect, so don't judge on one effort. Try and budget for a year's newsletters, balancing the contents over the whole year, rather than showing off everything you do in every issue.

GOING INTO PRINT

Consider commissioning a freelance writer or editor to turn your text into an interesting read and bring an outsider's eye to the publication.

Be clear about what you want a publication to do for you, and who's going to read it.

Decide what level of enquiries generated by the newsletter justify continuing to publish. If you have a well-defined database, you may be able to team up with others trying to reach the same market. They may wish to advertise with you, or pay to include their material with your newsletter distribution.

How much to write?
A quick rule of thumb is about 450 words per A4 page, allowing for pictures, headlines and graphs. Allow about 300 words on the front page if you have a masthead (the newsletter title).

Mix long, medium and short pieces, with plenty of 50-word snippets of interesting facts to break up large chunks of text. Include a bullet point summary of larger pieces so the skimmers get the key messages.

A well-proven structure is news at the front, features in the middle and staff news plus short bits and pieces at the back:

Front
- masthead or cover with date/volume number, strapline (the newsletter of the XYZ Company) and logo
- teasers to entice readers inside (unnecessary with a four-page newsletter, but helpful when it grows to more pages)
- news – preferably topical
- contents list (except for a four-pager)

Middle
- in-depth background features on services, products or other aspects of the organisation

- profiles of people (key management and those with jobs in areas where you can highlight important issues such as quality control, customer or membership services, finance and marketing/sales)
- competitions
- information pieces

Back
- adverts
- information pieces

Story ideas

News
- all your press release subjects
- affiliations, subsidiaries, partnership ventures etc.
- amendments to existing products
- awards
- celebrity involvement with the company
- company involvement in sponsorships or charity events
- customer events
- expansion
- financial news
- general news and features on your industry sector
- new initiatives
- new ranges
- people appointments and news
- product or service updates
- seasonal news
- business-orientated sponsorships
- successes

Features
- case studies (with the client's approval)
- company or organisation information

- crossword/wordsearch
- editorial (for publications with more than 4pp)
- historical fact box
- in-depth product or service background features
- in-depth staff profiles
- interviews with staff and customers
- letters
- readers' special offers
- readers' response card (if you feature a lot of products or services)

Back
- contact details: how to get in touch with you
- space for mailing label, if needed
- publisher's name and address
- events calendar
- relevant staff or sponsorship sports and leisure news

Advertising prime positions
Plan to place key contents in prime positions or sell at a premium rate:

FC = front cover
IFC = inside front cover
OBC = outside back cover
IBC = inside back cover
DPS = double page spread

The publication production checklist

- ❑ Draw up agreed contents list
- ❑ Decide on pictures required
- ❑ Assess news value of stories
- ❑ Draw up page plan showing story, probable size (based on importance), pictures, intended position

- ❏ Determine print production schedule and agree relevant deadlines with the designer, contributors, photographers, repro house and printer
- ❏ Commission drawings and photos
- ❏ Commission/research stories and draft text
- ❏ Chase up contributors
- ❏ Chase up late pictures
- ❏ Run out text proofs
- ❏ Proof read and amend/record changes
- ❏ Run out clean proofs and distribute to all who need to approve text
- ❏ Get clearance of text signed off from all involved
- ❏ Make text amendments
- ❏ Run out second proof of all changes
- ❏ Proof second version and clear
- ❏ Check word count
- ❏ Adjust page plan for article size, according to word count and pictures
- ❏ Check that you are still on schedule and, if you are running late, amend your slot with the designer, repro house and printer
- ❏ Give final checked, cleared and proofed text to designer, along with all pictures, contents list and page plan. Text amendments after this point, usually classed as author's changes, incur charges on a 'per word' basis
- ❏ Return approved black and white page proof to designer
- ❏ Pass colour laser proofs. Changes after this stage will be expensive
- ❏ Receive cromalin proofs
- ❏ Return cromalins
- ❏ Deliver or check material has arrived at printer
- ❏ Check print run went according to schedule
- ❏ Check delivery/distribution from printer went ahead
- ❏ Organize distribution if you are DIY
- ❏ Evaluate reaction to publication and note comments for future issues
- ❏ Ensure contributors, news sources and subjects of features are thanked for their participation. Check and record the reaction they have had to their contribution

❑ Analyse contents for balance across geographical regions and subject matter. Arrange future features to compensate for any bias

❑ Obtain and send out competition prizes you have offered

❑ Obtain photos and other materials from printer. Return to owners

❑ Approve invoices from photographers, illustrators, printers, repro house, designer, outside editorial or proofing assistance or editorial consultancy, freelance journalists and distributor

Writing style guide

■ Over the whole document, make the average sentence length fifteen to twenty words

■ Use words your readers are likely to understand. (Do not use 'monies' or 'notwithstanding' if money and despite will do.)

■ Use only as many words as you need. (Instead of 'checking the accounts is an operation which is carried out on a regular basis' say 'the accounts are checked regularly'.)

■ Use the active voice unless there's a good reason for using the passive. (Instead of 'the figures were examined by us', say 'we examined the figures'.)

■ Use the clearest, crispest, liveliest verb to express your thoughts.

■ Use vertical lists to break up complicated text.

■ Reduce cross-references to the minimum.

■ In letters, avoid fusty first sentences and formula finishes. (Get rid of 'please find attached herewith' in favour of 'I attach'; remove 'please do not hesitate to contact the undersigned' in favour of 'please contact me'.)

■ Put accurate punctuation at the heart of your writing – punctuation is not an optional extra.

■ Plan before you write.

■ Organize your material in a way that helps readers to grasp the important information early and to navigate the document easily.

- Consider different ways of setting out information. Tables, diagrams and charts can save hundreds of words of text.
- Manage colleagues' writing carefully and considerately to boost their morale and effectiveness.
- Devote special effort to producing lucid and well-organised instructions. Test them with typical readers before you publish them.
- Use clear layout to present plain words in an easily accessible way – everyone hates small print and long paragraphs.

CHAPTER 12:

THE NEXT STEP

PR is a long-term process. As long as you are in business, you have a business reputation. It's up to you whether you manage that reputation or cast your fortune to the wind.

All you need to get your DIYPR plan up and running is in this book. However, small businesses are an incredibly diverse group. The techniques described are wide-ranging to suit many different businesses. What works for one, may be a waste of time for another. You will need to fine-tune PR with trial and error to discover the best results for your own business. What this book does give you is several years' head start in that process of discovery.

If you feel you'd benefit from a further motivational push from DIYPR training, consider asking your local business or trade association to contact us to arrange a DIYPR training course in your area. We can handle up to 18 business owners per session. Groups can split the costs of a day's training to kick-start your PR Plans, generate starter press lists and draft press releases.

Alternatively, the author can provide DIYPR consultancy for individual business owners, including a visit, press list research and customised press release. See the Source Appendix for contact details.

Hiring PR help

If you have been following your PR plan and generating effective press coverage, there will come a time when it all becomes too time-consuming. Dealing with demands made by the media is hard work. And all that publicity should mean your hands are full coping with expanding the business. That is when you need to consider hiring PR assistance.

As you are preparing to move up a league, it's not easy to hand over the reins of your business reputation to others. In reality, you will never really let the reins go, but there's a lot of time-consuming press release drafting and distribution, event organisation and planning that could be easily delegated to other efficient people.

Should you employ someone to handle your PR, or should you go to a PR agency? Would a freelancer be a better choice?

There are arguments in favour of all of these approaches. For the same price as retaining an agency on a regular contractual basis, you can employ an in-house person full time and possibly use them to help in other areas. However, an agency can field a whole team for bigger events, and you will have access to more experienced people for planning and any crises. A freelancer will devote less time to your business than a member of staff and has fewer resources than an agency. They will have no back-up when they are away, but a freelancer will probably work out as better value for money if you can cope during their absences. If you hate writing but want to beef up your press coverage, consider hiring a freelance journalist instead of a freelance PR person.

Ultimately, your decision will depend on your specific PR needs, the calibre of applicants you get, and the quality of agencies in your area.

Hiring in-house PR staff

Look for good writing skills and experience, someone who is highly computer-literate, as well as being good on the telephone and at face-to-face interviews. There's no use in hiring someone if you don't give them the tools to do the job. Budget for providing good computer equipment, fax modem, on-line facilities, subscriptions to press databases and membership of a PR organisation. Work out an annual PR budget for the newcomer to deploy.

They will need to be well organised and this is an area you should explore if you are thinking of hiring an ex-journalist. Without wanting to tar the whole profession with the same brush, it's fair to say that journalists brought up on daily deadlines sometimes find it hard to deal with plans and schedules stretching over weeks, months, possibly a year ahead. They need deadlines to spur them into action.

If writing skills are a priority because you want to launch a publication or a series of leaflets, as well as run a fortnightly press release programme, hire the journalist. No-one's perfect. Just make sure you plug the gaps by assigning someone who is well organised to help them keep longer-term projects on track.

It is important that you recruit someone who does not make you cringe at the thought of their being let loose on your behalf with the press. But don't knock someone for being ignorant of some aspects of your business. See how well they represented their previous employer and try and imagine how they will be in a few months' time.

Find out whether they are a member of a PR organisation or hold a relevant PR qualification or a qualification in a related discipline, like journalism, marketing or advertising. Qualifications vary widely from the purely theoretical to the well-grounded and comprehensive. Unless you are up to speed with current PR teaching standards, regard qualifications as less important than credibility and good experience.

Find out what experience they have had in PR and use your knowledge of dealing with the press and events to probe: what press contacts have they got? What is their best result from a press release? Can they tell you more about whatever they are claiming to have done? What sources do they use for their press lists? What sort of events have they helped to organize?

It is unlikely that someone with a sales background will have the necessary experience to function well in a PR role without any PR training. It's hard for sales people to step into an information role. They can easily antagonise press people by pressurising them with sales pitches. They will be told to buy advertising instead.

After you hire someone, be the figurehead for prestigious interviews and to approve press release text.

Hiring an agency

An agency can give you an entire team if you need it for a launch or special occasion. The agency does not go on holiday or off sick, but it's true to say that the people closest to your account are as vulnerable as any other human being.

An agency can man the phone round the clock, if necessary, and can field more experienced people on an 'as needed' basis. You can use their directors' expertise to help outline your overall strategy and cope with any tricky problems, allowing the account manager and executive to do the legwork. An agency will have a wider range of expertise, press contacts and skills than one person.

However, an agency will not necessarily be as committed as a dedicated employee. They often have problems maintaining consistent standards.

Basically, it's up to you to check out agency work and keep tabs on how well they do their job.

If you are searching for a PR agency, ask for recommendations. In particular, ask your press contacts to tell you which agencies are effective. To reduce travel expenses, choose PR companies in the same area, draw up a shortlist of three or four based on personal recommendations and your own research. The Institute of Public Relations and the PR Consultants Association (see Source Appendix) operate professional codes of practice and can give you lists of UK members in your area. In the US, the Media Distribution Services website contains a one-stop guide to the PR profession on www.prplace.com

Approach the shortlisted agencies and ask for their credentials: how they operate, examples of case studies and the services they provide. Find out whether there is a conflict of interest with other clients.

Make sure you meet the team that will be involved on your account: most agencies have someone who's brilliant at winning business; they tend to put them onto the pitch team regardless of whether they will be involved in the day-to-day running of the account. Ultimately, having confidence in the person handling your account on a day-to-day basis is the most important criterion for choosing an agency. You will need to probe the level of knowledge and the press contacts they have in your particular field.

Once you have seen the credentials, ask for an hour's presentation from the two leaders and be prepared to give both agencies a considerable amount of your time to brief them on the background to your business (see the PR Plan chapter questionnaire for the sort of information they will need). Tell them the budget you have available and make it clear that this is the maximum including expenses, so you can see who comes up with the best use of the money.

THE NEXT STEP

To make direct comparisons, see the agencies back-to-back. Look for an understanding of the brief and delivery of your key business objectives. Seek out the priorities. How well has the target audience been identified? Have they demonstrated knowledge of your business and your business sector? What is the plan of action? How many releases or events are they suggesting and are they well distributed to give you steady year-long coverage? How important will your account be to them?

There is one area in which some agencies shoot themselves in the foot: the way in which expenses and disbursements are handled. Unless you check out their standard policy, your first bill could be a nasty shock. Take up client references and ask around before you sign up.

Make sure you know what the retainer covers: is it based on a minimum number of hours committed to your business? What's the hourly rate? Is there a ceiling on the hours involved? Agencies routinely add 17-25% handling fees on suppliers.

Ensure you have a clear contract, with measurable goals the agency must reach. This could be the number of releases put out, the number of events organised, or the minimum acceptable level of press coverage. This last criteria has to have some flexibility, since the nature of press relations is somewhat erratic. But if you are getting a lot of excuses and few column inches, it's useful to have minimum levels to act as a contract breaker.

It is a good idea to have an initial six-month trial period before signing up for a year at a time. Six months allows enough time for results to start coming through. Most agencies will not go through the set-up process with their press contacts for a shorter period. Do not commit to more than a year and review each year to keep the agency on its toes. Key agency staff may change or your situation may alter.

Build in regular meetings to review progress. If you feel you are not getting energy, enthusiasm, commitment and hard work for your money, talk to them. If things do not improve, change them.

On the other hand, clients need to give the agency feedback and information and be willing to work with them to achieve the best results. You need to be open and honest about your business plans, spend time keeping the agency up to speed on new developments and willing to take their professional judgement on board.

Whatever you decide, keep checking the budget and the actual spend, and relate the figures back to equivalent advertising costs to get an idea of the value for money you are getting.

The freelance route

A PR freelancer who is experienced in your field may give you the best of both worlds. Choose a PR freelancer with a good range of press contacts in your area, or go for a journalist freelancer who is willing to do PR work and is already feeding in to your key target media. In the UK, the Institute of Public Relations and the National Union of Journalists Freelance Division (see Source Appendix) should be able to point you in the right direction.

A good freelancer will give you a more personal service, but should charge less than a full service agency. They ought to have more contacts and experience than all but higher-paid PR employees. At least, with a freelancer, you only pay for services when you need them.

Many of the questions which apply to a potential employee would be helpful when interviewing a potential freelance PR consultant.

THE NEXT STEP

Similarly, much of the 'hiring an agency' advice applies when drawing up a contractual relationship with a freelancer.

Good luck and prosperous business!

Whether you carry on DIY PR, go down the in-house road, take the PR agency route or go for a freelancer, may all your press releases be productive and generate lots of 'free' publicity.

APPENDIX:

USEFUL ADDRESSES

☎ = telephone ➤ = fax

PR & Related Organisations:
Institute of Public Relations (IPR):
The Old Trading House, 15 Northburgh Street, London, EC1V 0PR
☎ 0171 253 5151, ➤ 0171 490 0588
Public Relations Consultants Association (PRCA):
Willow House, Willow Place, Victoria, London, SW1P 1JH
☎ 0171 233 6026, ➤ 0171 828 4797,
British Association of Communicators in Business:
☎ 0171 378 7139, ➤ 0171 378 7140

Press Directories, Distribution and Related PR Services:
PIMS UK Ltd (press lists etc.)
☎ 0171 354 7047. e-mail: prservices@pims.co.uk
Two-Ten Communications, (press lists etc.)
☎ 0171 490 8111, ➤ 0171 490 1255. e-mail: info@twoten.press.net
PR Planner, (press lists etc.)
☎ 01494 797260
Willings Press Guide:
☎ 01342 335872. Website: www.reedinfo.co.uk

APPENDIX

Advance Feature Search (forthcoming press features)
☎ 01296 428585. e-mail advance@themetree.co.uk
BRAD (advertising rates directory)
☎ 0171 505 8273
Foresight (future events lists)
☎ 0171 405 4455. e-mail: info@profilegroup.co.uk
Durrants (press cuttings service):
☎ 0171 588 3671
Romeike & Curtice (press cuttings service):
☎ 0181 882 0155 or 0800 289543
Tellex Monitors: (broadcast monitoring service)
☎ 0171 490 1447
National Union of Journalists (NUJ) Freelance Division:
☎ 0171 278 7916. e-mail: nuj@mcr1.poptel.org.uk
net.cut (Internet monitoring service)
☎ 0800 289 543
Hollis Directories (PR directories)
☎ 0181 977 7711. e-mail: hollis@hollis_pr.demon.co.uk
PR Week (weekly PR newspaper)
☎ 0171 413 4372

UK Marketing and Related Organisations

British Consultants Bureau,
1 Westminster Palace Gardens, 1-7 Artillery Row, London, SW1P 1RJ
☎ 0171 222 3651, ➤ 0171 222 3664
British Direct Marketing Association,
Grosvenor Gardens House, 35 Grosvenor Gardens, London, SW1W 0BS
☎ 0171 630 7322, ➤ 0171 828 7125.
British Institute of Management,
Management House, Cottingham Road, Corby, Northants, NN17 1TT
☎ 01536 204222, ➤ 01536 201651.
Chartered Institute of Marketing,
Moor Hall, Cookham, Maidenhead, Berks, SL6 9HQ
☎ 01628 524922, ➤ 01628 531381

**Communication Advertising and Marketing Education
(CAM) Foundation,**
Abford House, 3rd Floor, 15 Wilton Road, London, SW1V 1NJ,
☎ 0171 828 7506, ➤ 0171 976 5140.
Design Business Association, 29 Bedford Square, London, WC1B 3EG,
☎ 0171 631 1510, ➤ 0171 580 2338.
Direct Marketing Association (UK) Ltd,
Haymarket House, 1 Oxendon Street, London, SW1Y 4EE,
☎ 0171 321 2525, ➤ 0171 321 0191.
Institute of Customer Care,
St John's House, Chapel Lane, Westcott, Surrey, RH4 3PJ,
☎ 01306 876210, ➤ 01306 888910.
Institute of Management Consultants,
32-33 Hatton Garden, London, EC1N 8DL
☎ 0171 242 2140, ➤ 0171 830 4597.
Institute of Sales and Marketing Management,
31 Upper George Street, Luton, Beds, LU1 2RD
☎ 01582 411130, ➤ 01582 453640.
Institute of Sales Promotion,
Arena House, 66-68 Pentonville Road, Islington, London, N1 9HS
☎ 0171 837 5340, ➤ 0171 837 5326.
Management Consultancy Information Service,
32 Blenheim Avenue, Gants Hill, Ilford, Essex, 1G2 6SQ
☎ 0181 554 4695.
Marketing Society,
Derwent House, Stanton House, 206 Worple Road, London, SW20 8PN
☎ 0171 879 3464, ➤ 0171 879 0362.
Marketing Guild,
1 Houghton Court, Houghton Regis, Beds, LU5 5UX.
☎ 01582 864913
Sales Promotion Consultants Association,
PO Box 1578, London, E1 9FR
☎ 0171 702 8567, ➤ 0171 702 8570.

APPENDIX

Women in Direct Marketing,
Royal Mail House, 148-166 Old Street, London, EC1V 9HQ
☎ 0171 250 2365, ➤ 0171 250 2021.
Women in Marketing and Design, 9 Greenside Road, London, W12 9JQ
☎ 0181 749 3847, ➤ 0181 743 1715.

Small Business Organisations:
Networking Opportunities and/or Sources of Advice/Assistance

UK

150 Local Enterprise Agencies offer business advice: find which one is
nearest: ☎ 01234 354055.
238 Business Links in England offer business services: ☎ 0345 567765
Business Connect in Wales: ☎ 0345 969798
Business Shops in Scotland: ☎ 0800 787878
DTI's Guide to Help for Small Firms (URN 95/777):
free ☎ 0171 510 0169
The DTI's Enterprise Zone web site only contains links to other UK-
based web sites that are genuinely useful to SMEs. The DTI web site can
be accessed on http:// www.dti.gov.uk
Training & Enterprise Councils business advice and training
(England and Wales) ☎ 0114 259 4776.
Local Enterprise Companies in Scotland:
Scottish Enterprise ☎ 0141 248 2700 or Highland & Islands Enterprise
☎ 01463 234171.
The Prince's Youth Business Trust: ☎ 0171 543 1234.
The Prince's Scottish Youth Business Trust: ☎ 0141 248 4999
Tax, VAT and National Insurance joint helpline ☎ 0345 143 143 and
enquiries for their free "Starting Your Own Business" booklet
Inland Revenue self-assessment response line: ☎ 0345 161514
ADAS the food, farming and leisure consultancy advises farmers and
rural businesses in England and Wales. ☎ 01865 842742.

British Coal Enterprise Ltd: ☎ 01623 826833, ➤01623 826800

Inner Cities Central Unit: (DTI): ☎ 0171 215 6703, ➤ 0171 215 6055

Crafts Council: ☎ 0171 278 7700, ➤ 0171 837 6891

Small Business Information Centre (Ireland):
☎ 011 660 2244, ➤ 011 660 5095

Association of British Chambers of Commerce: ☎ 0171 222 1555

Association of Independent Businesses:
☎ 0171 371 1299, ➤ 0171 602 1922

Federation of Self-Employed and Small Businesses:
☎ 01253 720911, ➤ 01253 714651

Forum of Private Business: ☎ 01565 4467, ➤ 01565 650059

Home Office Club: ☎ 0502 511922, ➤ 0502 511923

Institute of Small Business Affairs: ☎ 0113 2832600, ➤0113 2833227

National Forum of Small Business Clubs: ☎ 0161 268 0085

Small Business Bureau: ☎ 01276 452010, ➤ 01276 451607

Stoy Centre for Family Business: ☎ 0171 486 5888, ➤ 0171 487 3686

British Franchise Association: ☎ 01491 578049

Franchise Centre: ☎ 0161 877 7788

Franchise Development Services Ltd: 01603 620301

Franchise World: ☎ 0181 767 1371

Telecottage Association: ☎ 0145 383 4874 or 0800 61600

National Association of Teleworkers: ☎ 01404 47467, ➤ 01404 46598

City Business Library: ☎ 0171 638 8215

Business Information Network: ☎ 0171 323 7499, ➤ 0171 323 7453

British Library: ☎ 01937 546023, ➤ 01937 546333

APPENDIX

Useful Online Services:

(It's also worth checking out some of the on-line US sites listed further on for good business advice, especially on marketing)

Dun & Bradstreet's on-line credit checking and direct marketing databases at http://www.dunandbrad.co.uk.

Accommodation booking: http://www.netxtra.co.uk/accom/ is an accommodation search engine allowing you to search a database of more than 50 countries and book a room using an online registration form.

Exporting: http://www.sitpro.org.UK/index.html is the DTI-sponsored Simpler Trade Procedures Board site with fact sheets, news and links to other relevant sites.

E-Mailed reminders: http://calendar.stwing.upenn.edu is the site for Remind U-Mail, a free of charge text-based site that will e-mail you with the reminders you've set up in advance in your Business information sources on the Internet: http://www.dis.strath.ac.uk/business/

CBI http:// www.cbi.org.uk - gives businesses access to updated policy news, trend surveys and events

Federation of Small Businesses at www.businessworld.co.uk

The International Organisation for Standardisation at www.iso.ch

UK Women's Business Associations

British Association of Women Entrepreneurs: ☎ 0171 722 0192

Women in Business: ☎ 01276 452010, ➤ 01276 451607

Women Returners' Network: ☎ 0171 388 3111, ➤ 0171 387 7324

UK Federation of Business and Professional Women:
☎ 0171 938 1729, ➤ 0171 938 2037

Network: ☎ 0181 963 1481, ➤ 0181 961 7468, e-mail:
netwomen@enterprise.net

Republic of Ireland Business organisations:

Craft Council of Ireland: ☎ 011 679 7368, ➤ 011 679 9197

Small Firms Association (SFA): ☎ 011 877 9801, ➤ 011 677 7823

Business Information Centre: ☎ 011 873 3996, ➤ 011 872 1451

Central Statistics Office: ☎ 011 676 7531, ➤ 011 668 2221

Chambers of Commerce of Ireland:
☎ 011 661 2888, ➤ 011 661 2811

European Business Institute: ☎ 011 676 8804, ➤ 011 676 8805

USA PR and Business organisations:

American Express Small Business Exchange:
http://www.americanexpress.com/smallbusiness

American Institute of Small Business: ☎ 800 328 2906

American Marketing Association, the world's largest association of marketing professionals. ☎ 800-AMA-1150 or www.ama.org

Crain Communications Inc: has an online directory of NY-related business information at http://www.crainsny.com

Dun & Bradstreet D&B Marketplace CD-ROM database of businesses is pricey but fairly comprehensive ☎ 800-590-0065, www.imarket.com. Similarly, have a look at Business USA CD-ROM ☎ 800-624-0076, www.lookupusa.com

Edward Lowe Digital Library contains a searchable database of smallbiz information http://www.lowe.org/smbiznet/index.htm

Entrepreneur Magazine's Small Business Square
http://www.entrepreneaurmag.com

Homeworks Home Page: advice on starting a business
http://homeworks.com

Luce Press Clippings: Toll-free 1-800-528-8226

Inc. Online http://www.inc.com/Inc.Online

APPENDIX

International Association of Business Communicators:

Microsoft's Smallbiz site: http://www.microsoft.com/smallbiz/

PR Web allows you to post press releases and search press releases on keywords: see how the pros do it at http://www.prweb.com. The site includes an online press release factory and for an extra fee, your releases can be distributed by PR Newswire (see below).

PR Newswire is the leading source of full text news for the media and the financial community. You can post press releases here for a fee: http://www.prnewswire.com

The National Federation of Independent Business at www.nfibonline.com

US Small Business Administration: federal aid and assistance for small businesses: http://www.sbaonline.sba.gov/

Your Company magazine's online pages: http://www.pathfinder.com/money/yourco/

Women in Business

The Online Women's Business Centre, part of the US Small Business Administration, contains a state-by-state list of resources at www.onlinewbc.org

Women's Connection focuses exclusively on women's issues and attracts over a million hits a month. Follow the site to see how you could tailor your approach to fit in. http://www.women.connect.com

INDEX

INDEX

complaints as opportunities, 39
contacts database, 29, 30, 59-61
corporate hospitality, 62-63
corporate identity, 63-64
customer profile, 40
customer service, 50
customers, 39-40, 43, 50

Dangers of growth, 48
databases, 42, 59-61
delegation, 48
design, 63-64
direct mail, 60
direct response mail, 42
Dun & Bradstreet, 61

Editorial, 83, 84-85
events, 65
exclusive writing, 99
exhibitions, 42, 65-66
expansion, 48, 148-151
expert comment, 97

Fairs, 42, 65-66
family, 5, 8-16, 49
faxes and the press, 113
features editor, 98
features pages, 98-100
financial information, 66-67
five golden rules, 117-127
five Ps, 41
five Ws, 119-123, 167-168
flyers, 67
freelance journalists, 194
friends, 5, 8-16, 49

INDEX

INDEX

PRESS RELEASE